Advent of the Savior

Advent of the Savior
A Commentary on the Infancy Narratives of Jesus

Stephen J. Binz

A Liturgical Press Book

THE LITURGICAL PRESS
Collegeville, Minnesota

	2	3	4	5	6	7	8

Library of Congress Cataloging-in-Publication Data

Binz, Stephen J., 1955–
    Advent of the Savior : a commentary on the infancy narratives of
Jesus / Stephen J. Binz.
        p.   cm.
    ISBN 0-8146-2410-3
    1. Infancy narratives (Gospels)   2. Bible.   N.T.   Matthew I–II—
Criticism, interpretation, etc.   3. Bible.   N.T.   Luke I–II—
Criticism, interpretation, etc.   I. Title.
BS2575.2.B5   1996
226.2'06—dc 20   96-12788
                                                                             CIP

Contents

Abbreviations

Gen—Genesis
Exod—Exodus
Lev—Leviticus
Num—Numbers
Deut—Deuteronomy
Josh—Joshua
Judg—Judges
Ruth—Ruth
1 Sam—1 Samuel
2 Sam—2 Samuel
1 Kgs—1 Kings
2 Kgs—2 Kings
1 Chr—1 Chronicles
2 Chr—2 Chronicles
Ezra—Ezra
Neh—Nehemiah
Tob—Tobit
Jdt—Judith
Esth—Esther
1 Macc—1 Maccabees
2 Macc—2 Maccabees
Job—Job
Ps(s)—Psalm(s)
Prov—Proverbs

Eccl—Ecclesiastes
Song—Song of Songs
Wis—Wisdom
Sir—Sirach
Isa—Isaiah
Jer—Jeremiah
Lam—Lamentations
Bar—Baruch
Ezek—Ezekiel
Dan—Daniel
Hos—Hosea
Joel—Joel
Amos—Amos
Obad—Obadiah
Jonah—Jonah
Mic—Micah
Nah—Nahum
Hab—Habakkuk
Zeph—Zephaniah
Hag—Haggai
Zech—Zechariah
Mal—Malachi
Matt—Matthew
Mark—Mark
Luke—Luke

John—John
Acts—Acts
Rom—Romans
1 Cor—1 Corinthians
2 Cor—2 Corinthians
Gal—Galatians
Eph—Ephesians
Phil—Philippians
Col—Colossians
1 Thess—1 Thessalonians
2 Thess—2 Thessalonians
1 Tim—1 Timothy
2 Tim—2 Timothy
Titus—Titus
Phlm—Philemon
Heb—Hebrews
Jas—James
1 Pet—1 Peter
2 Pet—2 Peter
1 John—1 John
2 John—2 John
3 John—3 John
Jude—Jude
Rev—Revelation

Preface

Advent is the season in which we reread and relive the experience of ancient Israel as it longed for the Messiah and the dawn of salvation. By attuning our lives to the Scriptures that anticipate and describe the first coming of the Savior, we personally enter into the expectancy of our ancestors in faith and deepen our longing for his coming again.

These infancy narratives of Matthew and Luke are an Advent preparation for the coming of Christ, the One "who was, and who is, and who is to come" (Rev 4:8). He who was born into our world through the maternity of Mary, also comes to us in countless ways, and will come to us again in the fullness of his glory.

Perhaps the best analogy for the Advent season is the feminine experience of pregnancy in preparation for birth. Advent is a time of expectant longing and joyful anticipation. We wait for movements and the stirrings of new life. In the midst of gloom and pain, we wait and hope.

Advent is also an opportunity to explore the darkness and gloominess of our world and our lives. The significance of Christ's coming to us depends on our understanding of the darkness that he dispels. By reflecting on the shadows and pains within our experience and that of others, we open our lives to watch and stand ready for the working of God. By struggling with these realities, we open them to the possibility of redemption celebrated in the coming of the Savior.

The gradually increasing light of the season, represented by the Advent candles and the seasonal lights on our streets and in our homes, represents the emerging light of Christ. He is the One who will shine on those in darkness, the light for the nations, the bright star that shines in the night, the dawning light of salvation that guides our feet on the path of peace.

In this season of watchful longing, we must ask ourselves, "What are our deepest yearnings?" Advent is the time to explore this question. It is the time to move gradually from longing to hope. By coming to understand more deeply what God has already done for us in sending us our Savior, we are able to deepen our hope for the certain coming of Christ to us. The Advent prayer of the early Church, "Come, Lord Jesus!" is still answered in new and surprising ways.

This commentary on the infancy narratives is intended especially for adult education and Bible study groups and for personal study and reflection on the Advent and Christmas texts. Like all who study the infancy narratives, I am indebted to the work of many others, especially for the monumental work of Raymond E. Brown, *The Birth of the Messiah*. In addition, I am grateful for and commend to you the works of Matthean commentators, Fred B. Craddock, Daniel J. Harrington, John P. Meiers, and Benedict T. Viviano, as well as the works of Lukan commentators, Joseph A. Fitzmeyer, Eugene LaVerdiere, Jerome Kodell, Luke Timothy Johnson, and R. J. Karris.

I am grateful for the staff of Little Rock Scripture Study, especially for the editorial suggestions of Cackie Upchurch and the video production that accompanies this work produced by Lilly Hess, and for the management and editorial staff of The Liturgical Press.

I dedicate this work to my bishop, Andrew J. McDonald, for his constant and supportive encouragement of Catholic Bible study over the past quarter century of his episcopacy, and to John Paul II, Pope of the New Advent.

STEPHEN J. BINZ

Introduction to the Infancy Narratives

In their infancy narratives, Matthew and Luke have given us two magnificent overtures to their accounts of the saving ministry of Jesus Christ. These simple yet profound narratives express the basic truths about the divine and human mystery of Jesus Christ. A faith-filled study of these two birth accounts strives for a deeper understanding of the stories in all their details, while at the same time deepening a sense of awe and wonder at the marvelous miracle of the advent of the Savior.

These four chapters have an importance for Christians far greater than their length may indicate. The art, poetry, prayer, hymnody, and doctrine arising from these infancy narratives have enriched the lives of believers through the centuries. A reflective study of each account will lead to a richer appreciation of the Christian faith and practice which have radiated from these writings of Matthew and Luke.

It is not the objective of this commentary to speculate about the process whereby these narratives were handed down and developed within the early Church. Though we should assume that these accounts are rooted in history, their development into the Gospel narratives is a subject far beyond the scope of this commentary. The principal objective of this commentary is to interpret the Gospel texts as they have been given to us by the inspired authors. The commentary will attempt to illuminate what the evangelists teach us about the identity of Jesus and about the meaning of his coming.

The infancy narratives point backward to the whole history of Israel, and they point forward to the entire Gospel of Jesus Christ, culminating in his death and resurrection and the apostolic mission of the Church. By directing us back to the people and events of the old covenant and by leading us forward to the main body of the Gospel, these narratives are truly a proclamation of the good news of salvation for all of humanity.

These opening chapters from Matthew and Luke form a bridge linking the Old and New Testaments. Through recounting the real people and actual places associated with the advent of Jesus, the evangelists situate his coming within the long history of salvation through which God had already been at work. Yet, the evangelists also demonstrate that Jesus embodied the whole history of Israel and brought that saving history to its climactic conclusion.

By showing echoes of Israel's history throughout their accounts, the evangelists demonstrate that the Old Testament finds its fulfillment in the person and the work of Jesus. Through offering insights into the Old Testament in light of the New, Matthew and Luke demonstrate that Jesus is the heir of all God's revelation given in the Hebrew Torah, prophets, and writings.

These infancy narratives also form prologues for each of the Gospels. They anticipate the proclamation of the saving Gospel in the life, death, and resurrection of Christ. Indeed, they contain the Gospel message—proclaiming the identity of Jesus as the Christ and Son of God and inviting all to come to salvation in him.

The earliest preaching of the disciples centered on the death and resurrection of Jesus Christ. In his glorification the Church came to realize most fully his identity and the meaning of his life in God's saving plan. Because of God's revelation made known through the Holy Spirit, Paul was able to proclaim "the gospel about his Son, descended from David according to the flesh, but established as Son of God in power according to the spirit of holiness through resurrection from the dead, Jesus Christ our Lord" (Rom 1:3-4).

Yet, Jesus did not become the Christ and Son of God at his resurrection. The Gospels demonstrate that the resurrection unveiled an identity that was already there. The Gospel of Mark proclaims the revelation of Jesus' identity through the Holy Spirit at his baptism. Matthew and Luke, however, declare that Jesus was Christ, Lord, and Son of God from the very beginning of his earthly life, from his conception by the Holy Spirit in the womb of the Virgin Mary.

Through the newborn Christ in the crib and the crucified Christ on the cross, the good news of salvation is proclaimed. This "infancy gospel" produces the same responses as the good news of Christ's death and resurrection. Some believed it and came to worship—the magi and the shepherds; others rejected it. Herod, the chief priests, and the scribes, who seek the death of the newborn, anticipate the passion of Christ and the persecution of his disciples. Indeed this child will be, as Simeon says, "a sign that will be contradicted."

It is best to study the infancy accounts of Matthew and Luke separately, not seeking to harmonize their different details. Each evangelist gives us a different portrait of Jesus, selecting and adapting details from the apostolic tradition in his own way. Each directs us back to the Old Testament and forward into his Gospel in a way that makes each Gospel a unique contribution to our fuller understanding of Jesus Christ.

Only Matthew records the dreams of Joseph, the coming of the magi, the star, the murder of the children by Herod, and the flight into Egypt. Only Luke gives us the annunciation to Mary, the visit to Elizabeth, the journey to Bethlehem for the census, the search for shelter and birth in the manger, the visit of the shepherds, and the presentation in the Temple.

Yet, while the details differ, both give a remarkably similar message about who Jesus is and the meaning of his coming. Both declare that Joseph is of the line of David and that Mary and Joseph are legally engaged but have not yet come to live together. In both, an angelic announcement reveals that the conception of the child is not through human intercourse, but through the Holy Spirit; that he is to be named Jesus; and that he is to be the Savior. In both accounts the birth of Jesus was in Bethlehem, during the days of Herod, and his early life was spent in Nazareth. It is generally agreed that Matthew and Luke wrote their accounts independently of each other, but drew from a common tradition remembered within the community of faith.

By knowing the Scriptures, we know Christ. Like all the inspired literature of the Bible, the infancy narratives are a call to deeper faith. Though these narratives may be legitimately excerpted from the Bible and studied individually, they call us to further reading and study. These prologues urge us to continue to study the Gospels which they introduce as well as the other Christian writings which expand their message. Yet these narratives also convince us of the necessity to study the Old Testament. It is only in studying the writings of our ancestors in Israel that the richness of God's plan of salvation can be understood.

11

The Infancy Narrative According to Matthew

The infancy account of Matthew is the ideal beginning of the New Testament. It demonstrates, on the one hand, that the coming of Jesus is in continuity with the whole of the Old Testament, and on the other hand, that the coming of Jesus Christ is a strikingly new event, remarkably unlike anything that God has done before.

The evangelist was a Jewish Christian, writing to give instruction and encouragement for both Jews and Gentiles. The whole Gospel stresses the connections between the story of Israel and the life of Jesus and the fulfillment of the Old Testament in Christ. Besides numerous citations from the Old Testament, the Gospel depicts Jesus as the great Teacher, who like Moses, is tested in the desert and delivers his teaching on the mountain. In fact, after the infancy narrative which serves as a prologue, the Gospel consists of five sections or "books" paralleling the five books of the Torah.

Matthew's infancy narrative begins with a genealogy followed by five episodes, each centered around a citation from the Old Testament. The narrative is told in a way which shows the fulfillment of saving history and of God's Word in the coming of Jesus. The Old Testament citations reinforce the understanding that the whole life of Jesus completed God's plan.

The coming of Christ occurs against the background of Israel's epic history. Each of the principal periods of salvation history is echoed in the infancy narrative. The period of the patriarchs is recalled as Jesus is described as son of Abraham and as Joseph is portrayed against the background of Joseph the dreamer in the Book of Genesis. The period of the Exodus is evoked in the parallels between the birth of Jesus and the birth of Moses, in the departure from Egypt by the family of Jesus, and in the magi and star account which is shaped on the story of Balaam in the Book of Numbers. The era of the monarchy is remembered as the promises given to David and his descendants are shown to be fulfilled in Jesus, the Messiah. Finally, the age of the exile is evoked as the weeping of Rachel recalls the banishment of God's people from the land.

The titles of Jesus given in Matthew's infancy account—Messiah, Son of God, Savior, and Emmanuel—anticipate the understanding of Jesus developed throughout the Gospel. The infant, born of the line of David and conceived by the Holy Spirit, will be acclaimed as Messiah and Son of God. The newborn Savior will save his people from their sins. The child called Emmanuel, "God is with us," will indeed be with his people always.

Matthew's infancy account presents Jesus as the true king. He is the messianic king, the king of the line of David, a humble shepherd king, and the royal Son of God. Through the kingship of Jesus, God's reign is established among the people. The presentation of Jesus as king in the infancy narrative develops most fully in Matthew's account of the passion and resurrection. From the manger to the cross Matthew develops the identity of Jesus as the royal Son of God.

The kingly rule of Jesus is strongly contrasted with the reign of King Herod. The kingship of Jesus is righteous, humble, committed to the salvation of God's people, even to the point of his own sacrificial death. Herod's kingship is egotistical, deceptive, committed to maintaining his own power, even to the point of destroying others.

Matthew's narrative demonstrates two responses to the kingship of Jesus that will be developed throughout the Gospel: the choice to obey the divine will and to worship Jesus (Joseph and the magi) and the choice to oppose God's will and try to destroy Jesus (Herod and the chief priests and scribes). The response of worship and obedience is developed in the Jewish and Gentile disciples of Jesus; the response of opposition continues in the religious leaders and their cruel persecution of Jesus. Yet, as Herod's opposition and attempts to kill Jesus ultimately fail to destroy Jesus, so the religious leaders will fail because of God's sovereign action on behalf of Jesus in the resurrection.

Matthew may well be describing his own role within the Christian community when he describes the role of a scribe: "Every scribe who has been instructed in the kingdom of heaven is like the head of a household who brings from his storeroom both the new and the old" (13:52). Indeed this is what Matthew does in his Gospel; he shows the meaning of Jesus for the ancient Jews and for the Gentiles from all the

MATTHEW 1:1-17 THE GENEALOGY OF JESUS

nations. The "old" is the Tradition and Scriptures of ancient Israel; the "new" is the Tradition and emerging Scriptures of Christianity.

Through the angels and prophets of his infancy narrative, Matthew shows that the new events have happened according to God's plan and initiative. Indeed all Christian teachers and writers must understand and express the reality that the new events are all rooted in the old. The advent of the Savior is the fulfillment of God's plan made known through the history of Israel as well as the beginning of God's new design for the unity of Jews and Gentiles, for the salvation of all the nations.

Matthew 1:1-17 The Genealogy of Jesus

¹The book of the genealogy of Jesus Christ, the Son of David, the son of Abraham.

²Abraham became the father of Isaac, Isaac the father of Jacob, Jacob the father of Judah and his brothers. ³Judah became the father of Perez and Zerah, whose mother was Tamar. Perez became the father of Hezron, Hezron the father of Ram, ⁴Ram the father of Amminadab. Amminadab became the father of Nahshon, Nahshon the father of Salmon, ⁵Salmon the father of Boaz, whose mother was Rahab. Boaz became the father of Obed, whose mother was Ruth. Obed became the father of Jesse, ⁶Jesse the father of David the king.

David became the father of Solomon, whose mother had been the wife of Uriah. ⁷Solomon became the father of Rehoboam, Rehoboam the father of Abijah, Abijah the father of Asaph. ⁸Asaph became the father of Jehoshaphat, Jehoshaphat the father of Joram, Joram the father of Uzziah. ⁹Uzziah became the father of Jotham, Jotham the father of Ahaz, Ahaz the father of Hezekiah. ¹⁰Hezekiah became the father of Manasseh, Manasseh the father of Amos, Amos the father of Josiah. ¹¹Josiah became the father of Jechoniah and his brothers at the time of the Babylonian exile.

¹²After the Babylonian exile, Jechoniah became the father of Shealtiel, Shealtiel the father of Zerubbabel, ¹³Zerubbabel the father of Abiud. Abiud became the father of Eliakim, Eliakim the father of Azor, ¹⁴Azor the father of Zadok. Zadok became the father of Achim, Achim the father of Eliud, ¹⁵Eliud the father of Eleazar. Eleazar became the father of Matthan, Matthan the father of Jacob, ¹⁶Jacob the father of Joseph, the husband of Mary. Of her was born Jesus who is called the Messiah.

[17]Thus the total number of generations from Abraham to David is fourteen generations; from David to the Babylonian exile, fourteen generations; from the Babylonian exile to the Messiah fourteen generations.

The opening phrase of the New Testament, "The book of the genesis/genealogy" (biblos geneseos), evokes associations with the first book of the Hebrew Scriptures, Genesis. The opening book of the Bible uses this same phrase in reference to God's original creation (Gen 2:4 in the Greek Septuagint). What God is doing in Jesus Christ is a new beginning, a new creative action for the world.

This phrase also introduces the account of the origins or the genealogy of Jesus which follows. Here the evangelist demonstrates that Jesus is connected to all of the individual names listed and that in him the highest hopes of Israel are achieved. The three titles of Jesus that introduce the genealogy highlight his identity that will be developed throughout the Gospel.

"Christ" is the Greek word for the Messiah, the anointed king who was expected to fulfill the hopes of Israel. "Son of David" is a messianic title proclaiming Jesus' royal descent in the line of David. As the heir of David, Jesus completes the promises God made to David that his dynasty and his kingdom would endure forever (2 Sam 7:12, 16). "Son of Abraham" associates Jesus with the beginnings of God's covenant with Israel and to the promise that in his descendants all the nations of the earth shall find blessing (Gen 22:18).

To understand biblical genealogies the reader must understand their purpose. They are rarely concerned with mere biological descent. The purpose of this genealogy is to introduce the Gospel by showing how Jesus fits into and completes the plan of God's saving history which came before him. By tracing the lineage of Jesus back through the whole history of God's people, Matthew demonstrates that the coming of Jesus was designed by God and that Jesus was born at the climactic time in Israel's history.

For hearers of Matthew's Gospel the genealogy stresses that the beginning of the story of Jesus is the Old Testament. For Jewish Christians the genealogy shows them that the whole history of their people has been planned by God to move toward the Messiah. For Gentile Christians it shows that they cannot fully know Jesus Christ unless they know his ancestors in the Scriptures of Judaism.

Salvation history is here divided into three great epochs. The first period begins with Abraham and ascends to the high point of Israel's history, the kingship of David. Within this period, Jesus is shown to be related to the great patriarchs of Israel, including not only Judah but "his brothers." The twelve sons of Jacob connect Jesus to the whole of Israel, the twelve tribes who will be called to the kingdom by the twelve apostles of Jesus. The monarchy of David first joined the tribes together and confirmed their united destiny in the kingdom of Israel.

The second epoch begins with King David and descends to the low point of Israel's history, the exile in Babylon. Within this period is a list of corrupt Judean kings, described in the Scriptures as murderers, idolaters, and adulterers. Only Hezekiah and Josiah are described as faithful to God's law. By the time of the Exile, the people of Jerusalem have almost given up hope for a king who would realize their dreams.

The third period begins after the Babylonian Exile and ascends again to the goal of Israel's history, the coming of Christ. Except for the first two, Shealtiel and Zerubbabel, and the last two, Joseph and Mary, they are a collection of obscure people whose names never made it into the Jewish Scriptures. Yet through them the hope of God's people was restored as salvation dawned.

The three-times-fourteen pattern is the evangelist's demonstration that Jesus came when the time was right in God's providential plan. There were fourteen days from the new moon, the beginning of the Jewish month, to the full moon, the day of Israel's greatest feasts, Passover and Tabernacles. Thus David and Jesus are preceded by fourteen waxing generations, beginning with the new moon of Abraham and the darkness of the Exile. The moon in its full luminance represents the reign of David and the advent of Christ. It is also significant that the letters for David in Hebrew (d-w-d) have the numerical value of fourteen (4+6+4). Thus the pattern of the generations expresses the fact that Jesus is indeed the Messiah, the long-awaited Son of David.

It was even more common for the Jews at the time of Jesus to divide time into periods of sevens. Considering this division of history, Jesus was preceded by six periods of seven generations (three X fourteen). The reign of the Messiah opened the seventh period of seven, the period of fullness and completion. The advent of Christ marked the end of God's careful plan.

The inclusion of five women is unusual for biblical genealogies. Their mention indicates that each of them played a crucial role in the ongoing history of salvation. Yet, they seem unlikely choices to be included in the messianic lineage.

Tamar, a Canaanite, was left childless after the death of her husbands. She disguised herself as a prostitute and seduced her father-in-law Judah in order to bear a child. Rahab, another Canaanite, was a real prostitute who protected the spies of Israel when they came to Jericho. Ruth, a Moabite, traveled to Judah after the death of her Israelite husband and married Boaz in Bethlehem. Bathsheba, "the wife of Uriah," a Hittite, became a wife of King David after he shamefully impregnated her and arranged her husband's death.

Each of these women was considered an outsider, a foreigner. Their presence in the genealogy of Jesus foreshadowed the messianic mission which invited Gentiles as well as Jews into the kingdom of God. Each also had unusual marital histories that could be looked upon as scandalous and scornful. Their inclusion along with many corrupt and scandalous men in the genealogy prepared for the ministry of Jesus in which sinners and prostitutes entered the kingdom. Indeed, the universal Gospel of Jesus Christ breaks down the barriers between Jew and Gentile, male and female, saint and sinner.

The final woman in the genealogy is Mary. Like the other women, her marital situation is highly unusual and scandalous to outsiders. Despite their situations, all five of these women played an important role in God's providential plan to continue the lineage of the Messiah. Tamar continued the family line of Judah's son. Rahab made it possible for Israel to possess the Promised Land. Ruth gave birth to the grandfather of King David. Bathsheba made certain that her son Solomon succeeded David. Mary's response to God's unexpected plan enabled her to become God's greatest instrument and to bring the lineage of the Messiah to its fulfillment.

God works in unexpected ways. The genealogy gives us a preview of that peculiar collection of men and women who will follow Jesus and who will become the Church in which Matthew ministered. The sinful, scandalous, unknown, and marginalized people who will come into the kingdom and experience salvation in Christ are powerful witnesses that the Holy Spirit is at work.

The final names in the lineage of Jesus break the steady rhythm of the genealogical pattern. The shift that occurs in verse 16 shows that Matthew wanted to indicate that Joseph was not the biological father of Jesus. The virginal conception and birth of Jesus introduces something radically new in human history as the messianic age dawns.

Though Jesus was born of the royal line within Israel's history, as Messiah he concludes the final period of the old Israel and opens up the new era of God's saving plan.

Matthew 1:18-25 The Birth of Jesus

[18]Now this is how the birth of Jesus Christ came about. When his mother Mary was betrothed to Joseph, but before they lived together, she was found with child through the holy Spirit. [19]Joseph her husband, since he was a righteous man, yet unwilling to expose her to shame, decided to divorce her quietly. [20]Such was his intention when, behold, the angel of the Lord appeared to him in a dream and said, "Joseph, son of David, do not be afraid to take Mary your wife into your home. For it is through the holy Spirit that this child has been conceived in her. [21]She will bear a son and you are to name him Jesus, because he will save his people from their sins." [22]All this took place to fulfill what the Lord had said through the prophet:
[23]"Behold, the virgin shall be with child and bear a son,
    and they shall name him Emmanuel,"
which means "God is with us." [24]When Joseph awoke, he did as the angel of the Lord had commanded him and took his wife into his home. [25]He had no relations with her until she bore a son, and he named him Jesus.

Matthew's account leading to the birth of Jesus continues to tell us who Jesus is. He is Son of David, as the genealogy has shown; and he is, even more significantly, Son of God. Through Joseph's lineage Jesus is Son of David; through Mary he is begotten as Son of God. Through the legal paternity of Joseph the coming of Jesus is in continuity with Israel's history; through the virginal maternity of Mary his coming is totally new.

The narrative explains how Jesus is both Son of David and Son of God by describing the relationship of Mary and Joseph. The couple is between the two stages of Jewish marriage. The first stage is the formal exchange of consent, made at the home of the bride's father. The second stage, made some months or years later, is the solemn transfer of the bride to the house of the groom. The betrothal of Mary and Joseph is a legally contracted marriage, completed before they came to live together.

The miraculous conception of the child in the womb of Mary is the work of the Holy Spirit. In the Old Testament, God's spirit was described as God's life-giving, creative power. The spirit of God was associated with the work of creation, with the utterance of the prophets, and with the work of re-creation in the last days. In Mary the Holy Spirit acts in a way that continues yet surpasses the work of God's spirit throughout salvation history. The conception of Jesus shows the Holy Spirit at work in a new and ultimate way.

The reader knows more than Joseph who became aware of Mary's pregnancy before he learned its meaning and cause. Joseph knew that Mary was holy and honorable, yet he also knew that pregnancy could only be the result of either willing or forced relations with a man. Joseph had to decide whether or not to take his pregnant bride to his home.

Joseph is described as a "righteous man," one who lives according to the law of God and seeks to fulfill God's will in every respect. How could he show faithfulness to God's law and also devoted concern for Mary? According to the law given in Deuteronomy, he could have exposed her to the humiliation of a public procedure. Yet, he decided to shield her from shame by giving her the prescribed document of divorce privately.

Joseph's agonizing choice is cut short by God's revelation in a dream. By calling Joseph "son of David," the angel calls to mind the messianic prophecy made to Joseph's ancient ancestor David. Joseph will be the predetermined link which joins Jesus to the family of David. By taking Mary into his home, thus assuming public responsibility for the care of Mary and the child, and by giving the child a name, Joseph becomes the legal father of Jesus. In this way, the account explains how Jesus is able to be of the lineage of David though he was not the physical son of Joseph.

Through Joseph's compliant response to the divine will, Jesus is able to be called Son of David, and thus Messiah of Israel. Through the working of the Holy Spirit in Mary, Jesus is able to be called the Son of God. The angel says to Joseph: "She will bear a son and you are to name him Jesus." The complementary and obedient responses of Mary and Joseph are necessary for the coming of the Savior.

The name Jesus is the Greek form of the Hebrew name "Yeshua/ Joshua," popularly interpreted to mean "God saves." Because the name was given to him by God, it connects the name of Jesus with God's saving plan made known in the Scriptures. The great deliverer of God's people from bondage was Moses, yet it was Joshua who led Israel into the promised land. Joshua saved God's people from their enemies in the land; Jesus "will save his people from their sins." "His people" is the Church—all those Jews and Gentiles who will experience forgiveness through his life-giving death, a death whose power is continually available through the "blood of the covenant" shed "for the forgiveness of sins" (26:28).

The prophecy in verse 23, cited from Isaiah 7:14, was an oracle of hope given originally to the house of David in the eighth century before Christ. It referred to the coming birth of a king, one who would restore the glorious line of David and be a sign that God was with Israel. Since the kings of Judah never fulfilled the high ideals of these Emmanuel prophecies (especially Isaiah 7, 9, and 11) the expectation of a future, ideal messianic king grew stronger.

The Hebrew text calls the woman of the prophecy "the maiden." It may be assumed that the young woman was a virgin, though the Hebrew word does not specify virginity. However the Greek text of the Septuagint, the Old Testament text more familiar to the early Christians, calls the woman "the virgin." Her virginity makes it clear that her child would be a firstborn.

Each of the five fulfillment citations of Matthew's infancy account indicate that the advent of Jesus was foreordained by God and that his coming completed the expectations in the Old Testament. Though the ancient prophets could not have known the full meaning of their words in the divine plan, the early Christians and the inspired evangelist were able to recognize the texts as expressing God's plan for the coming of Jesus.

This text from Isaiah 7:14 expressed and fortified the early community's faith in the messianic identity of Jesus and his virginal conception. Through this text the Gospel proclaims that Jesus is the long-awaited Savior, that he was born of the Virgin Mary, and that in him God is with his people in a completely new way.

The name Emmanuel, "God is with us," completes the divine promise made to the patriarchs and prophets, "I will be with you." The great divide that separates God and his people is sin. Because Jesus saves his people from their sins, God's people are able to recognize the divine presence. The Emmanuel of the infancy narrative anticipates the end of the Gospel when Jesus proclaims "I am with you always" (28:20).

God's angel and God's Word explain to both Joseph and the reader the origin and the destiny of the Son of Mary. By obediently responding to all that God asked of him, Joseph became like a father

to Jesus—accepting as his own the child who would have been re-
garded as illegitimate, and naming the child Jesus.

Joseph took Mary into his home, though he did not have intercourse with her "until she bore a son." The Greek text emphasizes
that Mary conceived and gave birth to her son as a virgin, but it
does not affirm or deny marital relations after Jesus' birth.

Matthew 2:1-12 The Visit of the Magi

> [1]When Jesus was born in Bethlehem of Judea, in the days of
> King Herod, behold, magi from the east arrived in Jerusalem,
> [2]saying, "Where is the newborn king of the Jews? We saw his
> star at its rising and have come to do him homage." [3]When King
> Herod heard this, he was greatly troubled, and all Jerusalem
> with him. [4]Assembling all the chief priests and the scribes of
> the people, he inquired of them where the Messiah was to be
> born. [5]They said to him, "In Bethlehem of Judea, for thus it has
> been written through the prophet:
> > [6]'And you, Bethlehem, land of Judah,
> >   are by no means least among the rulers of Judah;
> > since from you shall come a ruler,
> >   who is to shepherd my people Israel.'"
> [7]Then Herod called the magi secretly and ascertained from
> them the time of the star's appearance. [8]He sent them to Bethle-
> hem and said, "Go and search diligently for the child. When
> you have found him, bring me word, that I too may go and do
> him homage." [9]After their audience with the king they set out.
> And behold, the star that they had seen at its rising preceded
> them, until it came and stopped over the place where the child
> was. [10]They were overjoyed at seeing the star, [11]and on entering
> the house they saw the child with Mary his mother. They pros-
> trated themselves and did him homage. Then they opened their
> treasures and offered him gifts of gold, frankincense, and myrrh.
> [12]And having been warned in a dream not to return to Herod,
> they departed for their country by another way.

The events in chapter two point backward to ancient Israel and
forward to the public life of Jesus. Each of the four episodes is related to a place associated with a key feature of salvation history.
Bethlehem harkens back to God's choice of David; Egypt recalls
God's decision to free Israel from bondage; Ramah is a reminder of
the captivity in Exile; Nazareth anticipates the life of Jesus. Each

21

episode also contains an Old Testament citation that contains the name of the place.

A strong contrast is established between the "newborn king of the Jews" and Herod, the wicked king of the Jews. Likewise a contrast is established between the Gentile strangers from the East who accept the newborn king and do him homage and the Jewish ruler who rejects him and seeks his death.

The reign of Herod the Great was noted for its murderous cruelty. He killed several of his own wives and many of his children. He was insanely distrustful and saw threats to his power everywhere. He had been appointed king of the Jews by the Romans, and he had taken upon himself the prerogative of the son of David by rebuilding the Temple in Jerusalem.

Herod felt threatened by the widespread expectation among the Jews of the coming messianic king, a new and greater David. So when news reached him that a child was born who was destined to be king, conflict was inevitable. That conflict with the rulers of Israel will continue until Jesus is mocked as king and crucified with the title attached to his cross—"King of the Jews."

Herod assembled the "chief priests and the scribes of the people." This council, the Sanhedrin of Jerusalem, appears positively here in that they know the prophecies of Scripture and thus they are able to tell Herod where the Messiah is to be born. Yet they are also "troubled" by the announcement along with "all Jerusalem." It is this group that will be the enemies of Jesus throughout his public life and will conspire to have him put to death. The leaders of the people know the prophecy, yet they refuse to recognize or accept his coming.

The Old Testament citation in verse 6 confirms that Bethlehem, the birthplace of David, was the expected birthplace of the Messiah. The passage consists primarily of an adapted use of Micah 5:1. Yet Matthew adds "by no means," emphasizing that though Bethlehem is small, her stature is great because Jesus has been born there. 2 Samuel 5:2 is the source for the last line: "You shall shepherd my people Israel." Like David, the messianic king will also be a good shepherd of God's people.

The magi, prompted by their observation of the star, arrive from an unknown land in the East. The word "magi" originally referred to a Persian priestly caste noted for their interpretation of dreams. Later it came to refer to any possessors of supernatural knowledge and power. Here they are probably astrologers who look to the movement of stars as a guide to human events and destiny.

Their origins, occupation, and questions suggest that they are Gentiles entering this thoroughly Jewish setting. Their astrological observations indicate that the Gentiles are able to see signs of the divine in creation. It was a common motif in antiquity that a new star marked the birth of a new ruler. These foreigners may have even been aware of the expectation that a worldwide ruler would come from Judah. Yet they had to consult the Jews about the messianic prophecies in order to unlock the more hidden mysteries of God.

Speculation about the astronomical identification of the star is endless. Theorists suggest that it may have been a supernova, a comet, or a conjunction of the planets. Yet it is the significance of the star at the Savior's birth that is most important. It is a sign rooted in the tradition of Israel, a heavenly sign that leads Gentiles on a search for a king who will rule the world.

The Old Testament tradition told of a star that would mark the coming of a messianic king. As Moses was leading the people to the promised land, he encountered a wicked king who, like the Pharaoh in Egypt, tried to destroy him. Balak, king of Moab, summoned from the East a famous seer named Balaam, in order to use his powerful knowledge against Moses and Israel. Balaam came with his two servants, but instead of cursing Israel, he gave a blessing on Israel's future. The oracle of Balaam refers to the emergence of the monarchy in Israel and states:

> "I see him, though not now;
>   I behold him, though not near:
> A star shall advance from Jacob,
>   and a staff shall rise from Israel" (Num 24:17).

The eastern seer frustrated the plans of the wicked king and proclaimed the coming of the messianic king, a king who would be announced by a star. Thus, the star was understood in the New Testament community to proclaim the birth of the long-awaited messianic king.

The rising star and the eastern visitors presenting gifts fit for a king suggest other passages from the Old Testament. Having proclaimed a redeemer for Jerusalem (Isa 59:20) Isaiah says:

> "Rise up in splendor! Your light has come,
>   the glory of the Lord shines upon you . . .

Nations shall walk by your light,
  and kings by your shining radiance . . .
  the wealth of nations shall be brought to you . . .
All from Sheba shall come
  bearing gold and frankincense,
  and proclaiming the praises of the LORD" (Isa 60:1, 3, 5-6).

The Isaian passage underlines the fact that the magi represent the Gentile nations who will experience the light of salvation in the Jewish Messiah.

The visit of the Queen of Sheba to the son of David, King Solomon, also prefigures the visit of the magi. She came from a distant land to visit the king in Israel, presenting him with gifts of gold, spices, and precious stones (1 Kgs 10:2). There she witnessed the renowned wisdom of Solomon and marveled at the Temple of God. Her visit prepared for all those who will experience the true wisdom and eternal temple in Jesus Christ. After her visit in which she received everything she desired, like the magi, she returned to her own country (1 Kgs 10:13).

Likewise Psalm 72 proclaims a son of David who will be honored by all the nations: "The kings of Arabia and Seba offer gifts." The adoration offered to Christ by the magi represents the homage of all the nations to be offered the Messiah: "May all kings bow before him, all nations serve him" (Ps 72:11). This association of the Son of David and the bright star in the New Testament tradition is further reflected at the end of the Book of Revelation in which the Risen Christ declares: "I am the root and offspring of David, the bright morning star" (Rev 22:16).

The contrast between Herod and the magi revolves around the threefold use of the Greek word for "do homage" (2:2, 8, 11). The term indicates a solemn bow or prostration rendered to a person of great dignity or authority. Herod feigns worship while the magi "prostrated themselves and did him homage." The action is shown to be the proper response to Jesus throughout the Gospel, and it will be the last act of the disciples at the end of the Gospel (28:17). The Gentile magi who gather at Christ's birth anticipate all the believers from all the nations who will be called to salvation through this Davidic king. Indeed this Son of David is also Son of Abraham in whom all the nations of the earth will be blessed.

The origins of Jesus point toward his destiny. During his public ministry some accepted him and did him homage; others rejected him and sought to put him to death. The disciples of Jesus met a similar response when they proclaimed the Gospel after the resurrection: Some accepted the saving good news, others opposed it and violently persecuted the community of faith. From his birth Jesus was destined to be the suffering Messiah, the Savior whose worldwide dominion brings salvation to all the nations.

Matthew 2:13-15 The Flight to Egypt

> [13]When they had departed, behold, the angel of the Lord appeared to Joseph in a dream and said, "Rise, take the child and his mother, flee to Egypt, and stay there until I tell you. Herod is going to search for the child to destroy him." [14]Joseph rose and took the child and his mother by night and departed for Egypt. [15]He stayed there until the death of Herod, that what the Lord had said through the prophet might be fulfilled, "Out of Egypt I called my son."

Three times in Matthew's narrative Joseph is instructed by an angel in a dream; three times he responds in obedience for the sake of the child and his mother. An angel appeared at decisive moments throughout the Old Testament to communicate the will of God; an angel will announce the resurrection of Christ at the end of Matthew's Gospel.

This account of Joseph resembles the great epic of Joseph the patriarch in the Book of Genesis (Gen 37–50). Joseph, the son of Jacob (also called Israel), was known as a dreamer and an interpreter of dreams. He saved his family from destruction by bringing Jacob-Israel from Canaan into Egypt. The New Testament Joseph relives the life of his Jewish ancestor through responding to God's revelation in his dreams. He too travels to Egypt to seek refuge for his family and he saved them from destruction.

Just as the advent of Jesus is a new genesis, so also it is a new exodus. The great epic of ancient Israel is continued with the story of Moses. The infancy narrative of Moses in the Book of Exodus foreshadows the infancy narrative of Jesus. The rescue of the infant Moses from the wicked Pharaoh prepares for the rescue of God's people through the later ministry of Moses. Likewise, the rescue of Jesus from the sinister king prepares for his later ministry of redeeming his people.

The Old Testament citation at the end of verse 15 is taken from Hosea 11:1, "When Israel was a child I loved him, out of Egypt I called my son." The prophet was speaking about the original Exodus from Egypt. He spoke of Israel collectively as God's adopted son. This filial relationship with God is experienced in its fullness by Jesus, the Son of God. The Exodus of Israel achieves its completion in Jesus as he relives and fulfills in his own life the history of his people.

The Gospel will go on to describe how the life of Jesus imitates and completes the formative experiences of Israel's life. Jesus will leave Egypt, pass through the water of the Jordan River in baptism, undergo trials and temptations in the desert, teach from the mountain, and establish the new covenant. His life is in continuity with Israel's history, yet he brings Israel to its climactic fullness. He is the new Moses, the renewed Israel, the eternal covenant, the Savior of his people.

The going down to Egypt and the call to come out of Egypt points back to Israel's past and forward to the end of Jesus' saving work. The Exodus from Egypt, the passage from slavery to freedom, is a foreshadowing of the death and resurrection of Jesus. The rulers of God's people in the infancy account were unable to destroy Jesus; so the rulers in the passion account are unable to destroy him. In both accounts Jesus is taken away, and he is brought back again. In the infancy narrative he is taken to Egypt and then brought back to the land where God's saving plan can be fulfilled. In the passion narrative his life is taken from him, and then he is brought back to life forever.

Matthew 2:16-18 The Massacre of the Infants

[16]When Herod realized that he had been deceived by the magi, he became furious. He ordered the massacre of all the boys in Bethlehem and its vicinity two years old and under, in accordance with the time he had ascertained from the magi. [17]Then was fulfilled what had been said through Jeremiah the prophet:
[18]"A voice was heard in Ramah,
   sobbing and loud lamentation;
Rachel weeping for her children,
   and she would not be consoled,
   since they were no more."

The narrative turns away from the Holy Family to report the rage of King Herod. His massacre of the innocent children of Bethlehem was a result both of his fear of a rival king and his rage at being deceived.

The word "deceived" carries the idea of being made to look foolish or mocked. The word appears again in the passion account when Jesus is "mocked" as king (27:29, 31, 41). When Herod, the fraudulent king of the Jews, is mocked, he responds by killing the innocent children of Israel. When Jesus the true king is mocked, he responds by accepting death, though he was innocent.

The massacre is entirely in keeping with Herod's ruthless character. He is the first of many who will try to prevent the advent of salvation by trying to kill its bearers. The death of the Holy Innocents prefigures not only the innocent death of Jesus but also the persecution of the disciples in the early Church and the long and glorious line of Christian martyrs.

Herod ordered the massacre of all the boys in the vicinity of Bethlehem, up to two years of age, so that there would be no escape. At the birth of Moses, the Pharaoh had commanded his subjects to kill "every boy that is born to the Hebrews" (Exod 1:22). The advent of salvation, for Israel and for the whole world, is accompanied by guiltless suffering and death.

The quotation is from the prophet Jeremiah 31:15. Rachel, the wife of Jacob-Israel, is imagined to be weeping for her children centuries after her death. In Genesis it is said that this matriarch of Israel died and was buried on the road to Ephrath, which is identified as Bethlehem (Gen 35:19). Tradition places her tomb there to this day.

The passage in Jeremiah refers to the deportation and captivity of the people of Israel. Ramah, a small town north of Jerusalem, was the place where the captives of Judah and Jerusalem were taken to begin their march into the Babylonian Exile (Jer 40:1). Rachel wept for the children of Israel, those who had been slaughtered by the enemy and those being taken into exile. As Jesus, the new Israel, goes into exile, Rachel is again imagined to be lamenting from her tomb for her slaughtered children.

Though the quotation in Matthew seems to indicate unrelieved suffering, in its context Jeremiah's prophecy expresses great joy and hope. Rachel is told to stop weeping because her children are returning from exile. This woeful lament is set in a chapter proclaiming a great future for Israel, including the promise of the new covenant (Jer 31:31-34).

The infant Jesus thus embodies the Exodus and the Exile, the two greatest periods of both suffering and vindication for the people of Israel. The Exodus from Egypt and the restoration after the exile in Babylon are events which, as the prophets proclaim, can be completed only in the coming of the Messiah. The future proclaimed by the prophets will be realized with the exodus of Christ's saving death and resurrection and the establishment of the new and everlasting covenant.

Matthew 2:19-23 The Return from Egypt

19When Herod had died, behold, the angel of the Lord appeared in a dream to Joseph in Egypt 20and said, "Rise, take the child and his mother and go to the land of Israel, for those who sought the child's life are dead." 21He rose, took the child and his mother, and went to the land of Israel. 22But when he heard that Archelaus was ruling over Judea in place of his father Herod, he was afraid to go back there. And because he had been warned in a dream, he departed for the region of Galilee. 23He went and dwelt in a town called Nazareth, so that what had been spoken through the prophets might be fulfilled, "He shall be called a Nazorean."

Though the principal actor in the Matthean infancy account is Joseph, the center of attention is the child Jesus and his mother Mary. The phrase "the child and his mother" is used repeatedly in all the events after the nativity (2:11, 13, 14, 20, 21). This focus on the messianic child along with his mother reflects the central role of the king's mother in the birth, enthronement, and reign of the Davidic kings of Judah.

The importance of the queen-mother is demonstrated throughout the Old Testament. The Book of Kings always mentions the name of the king's mother in the introduction to each reign in Judah. She had an official position in the kingdom and often kept her position even after her son's death. The queen-mother was enthroned with the king and enjoyed a position of great honor and dignity during his reign (Jer 13:18; 1 Kgs 2:19). Thus it is fitting that the mother of the Messiah should have a central role in the kingdom inaugurated by the coming of Christ.

The birth of Christ from Mary his mother, the attempt by Herod to destroy the child, and the intervention of God to save the child from death are also reflected in the images of Revelation 12. Here the woman who gives birth to the Messiah represents both the people of God in the Old Testament and the Christian Church. The birth of the Messiah is both his historical coming and his resurrection into glory. The dragon who waits to devour the child when he is born is all the powers that seek to destroy the Messiah and his reign.

Like Revelation 12, the Matthean account of Christ's birth looks backward to the history of struggle between the ruling powers of the world and the saving plan of God. It is a battle envisioned in the garden between the offspring of the dragon and the offspring of the woman (Gen 3:15) and continued in Israel's history with the struggle between the murderous Pharaoh and God's desire to liberate Israel. Like Revelation 12, the infancy narrative also looks forward to the ongoing conflict between the ruling powers and the messianic reign —a struggle which began with Herod's slaughter of the children, culminated in the crucifixion of Christ, and continued with the persecution of the Church.

The exile of Jesus and his family ends with the death of Herod. Like his ancestors exiled in Egypt and in Babylon and then freed to return to Israel, Jesus now returns with his family "to the land of Israel." The angel said, "those who sought the child's life are dead." This parallels God's words to Moses when God announced the death of Pharaoh and told Moses to return because all who sought his life were dead (Exod 4:19). That announcement freed Moses to begin his mission of freeing God's people and bringing them into the land of Israel. Likewise, the announcement of the angel freed the family of Jesus to go to the land of Israel, the place where Jesus would begin his saving work.

Yet those who sought his life only anticipate other ruling powers who will seek to frustrate the designs of God and put the Savior to death. Already the cruel Archelaus, the son of Herod the Great, ruled over Judea. So the family of Jesus settled in Galilee, the northern region of ancient Israel, where the reign of Herod Antipas, another son of Herod, enabled them to be slightly more secure.

Nazareth was a small village in Galilee, a place so obscure that it was never mentioned in the Old Testament. John's Gospel underlines its insignificance in the question of Nathanael, "Can anything good come from Nazareth?" (John 1:46). Yet, the evangelist demonstrates that the same prophetic Scriptures that spoke about the Davidic Messiah from Bethlehem also spoke about a Nazorean.

29

There is no single text in the Old Testament that contains the words quoted by the evangelist, "He shall be called a Nazorean." Thus establishing its biblical source has been a challenge through the ages. Since the phrase is not found in any single prophet, the evangelist uses the plural "prophets" instead of the usual singular. St. Jerome points out that the phrase is a summary of the prophets' teachings.

There are several different reasons why Jesus was called a Nazorean by the early Christians and why his followers were called Nazoreans (Acts 24:5). The most obvious reason is that he came from Nazareth. Yet, there are two other messianic associations of the term in the literature of Israel, both of which have implications for Jesus' identity.

Jesus is called a Nazorean also because he completes a line of Nazirites, those who were consecrated to God's service from the womb. The biblical figures described in this way in their birth narratives are Samson, Samuel, and John the Baptist. In addition, Jesus is called a Nazorean because he is the *netzer* (branch or shoot) prophesied in Isaiah 11:1. It was expected that the Messiah would be the budding shoot sprouting from the root of Jesse, the father of David.

Matthew shows us that clearly God is directing the history of the world's salvation. He shows how the advent of the Savior is in continuity with all that has come before him, yet also how his coming is a completely new act of God in human history. By looking backward into ancient Israel and looking forward into the ministry of Jesus, Matthew's infancy narrative shows how he "brings from his storeroom both the new and the old" (13:52). He shows us again how the "new" grows out of the "old," and the "old" finds a fuller expression in the "new."

Having completed the narrative of Christ's infancy, the evangelist invites the reader to continue the Gospel, to see how all the claims made for Jesus at his birth will be realized throughout his life. His words and deeds, death and resurrection will demonstrate that Jesus the Nazorean is indeed the Messiah and Son of God.

The Infancy Narrative According to Luke

Luke's infancy narrative serves as the overture to his two-volume work, the Gospel and the Acts of the Apostles. Through these works Luke demonstrates that the salvation first manifested in Jerusalem is destined to extend to all the world. The same Holy Spirit that overshadowed Mary to bring about the birth of Jesus also came upon Mary and the disciples at Pentecost to bring about the birth of the Church. Through the saving work of Jesus and his Church "all flesh shall see the salvation of God" (3:6).

Luke's writings show that Jesus is the center of the history of salvation. As Savior, Messiah, and Lord (2:11) he ushers in the time of salvation. He will bring deliverance from evil, infirmity, and the division caused by sin. He will heal the alienation that separates people from God and from one another. His saving power breaks down the barriers between people—Jew and Gentile, rich and poor, man and woman, mighty and humble. From the east, west, north, and south people will come to experience salvation (13:29), as Jesus comes "to save what was lost" (19:10).

From the perspective of a faith that had spread throughout the world, Luke brings his readers back to the Jewish world of Jerusalem to begin his Gospel. By weaving allusions, images, and language of the Old Testament throughout his text, the evangelist brings the reader into the world of ancient Israel. The prayers, hymns, poetry, stories, and prophecy of the infancy narrative enable the reader to recognize the old within this entirely new experience of God's grace. They reveal that God's universal plan was rooted in God's promises to Israel from the beginning.

The infancy narrative of Luke, like that of Matthew, looks backward to God's dealings and promises to Israel and forward to their extension and fulfillment in the life of Jesus and his Church. But because Luke's narrative is significantly longer than Matthew's, the reader is able to savor more fully the world of ancient Israel and so to be filled with a strong sense of anticipation for what is to come. The pervasive mood of Luke's narrative is expectation; the faithful people of God are waiting for the dawn of salvation.

The story of the Savior's advent in Luke begins with the coming of John the Baptist. He is the bridge between the old and new; he is the last of the prophets of Israel and the great precursor of Jesus, heralding the Messiah's coming. The other Gospels begin by describing John's adult ministry; only Luke describes his parents and infancy in anticipation of his public life.

Luke carefully structures his narrative by paralleling the origins of John and Jesus. The annunciation of John's birth is parallel to the annunciation of Jesus' birth. The response of John's mother is parallel to the response of Jesus' mother. The birth of John is parallel to the birth of Jesus. The circumcision and naming of John are parallel to those of Jesus. This artistic presentation is often compared to the two facing panels of a diptych, yet Luke makes it clear in each section who is the lesser and who is the greater. The elder will serve the younger.

As the Gospel and Acts continues, John the Baptist will "prepare the way of the Lord" (3:4). That "way" becomes Jesus' way to Jerusalem, the way of discipleship, the way of salvation, the new "Way" which is the Church. The preparation for salvation encouraged by John is a reminder to all readers of the need to make ready for the coming of the Lord.

The other great figure in the infancy account is Mary. Unlike Matthew's account in which the role of Joseph dominates, Luke's account focuses on the role of Mary. Because she was chosen to be the mother of the Lord, she is singularly bestowed with graces as God does great things for her. She is blessed among women and all ages will acknowledge her blessedness. She is the favored one of God, the one who will conceive and give birth to the Son of God.

Mary is also an inspiration and model for all who seek to follow in the way of Jesus. She generously and faithfully responds to God's working in her life. She believes that God's word will be fulfilled, and she surrenders her life to God's plans. She is grateful for the gifts God bestows upon her; she shows deep concern for the poor and lowly; and she hastens to help those in need. With trust Mary accepts what she cannot understand, and she ponders in her heart all that happens to her.

The Gospel, or "good news," proclaimed by Luke is impregnated with the joy of salvation. The angel who announced the birth of John to his father Zechariah said, "You will have joy and gladness and many will rejoice at his birth" (1:14); and Elizabeth declared that the infant in her womb "leaped for joy" (1:44) at the approach of Jesus in the womb of Mary. The angel Gabriel first greeted Mary with the word "Hail," which also means "Rejoice" (1:28); and the angel appeared to the shepherds to announce the birth of their Savior by proclaiming "good news of great joy" (2:10). Luke teaches all his readers how to wait for the Lord with joy, how to welcome his coming with joy, and how to receive his gift of salvation with joyful hearts.

Luke 1:5-25 Announcement of the Birth of John

> [5]In the days of Herod, King of Judea, there was a priest named Zechariah of the priestly division of Abijah; his wife was from the daughters of Aaron, and her name was Elizabeth. [6]Both were righteous in the eyes of God, observing all the commandments and ordinances of the Lord blamelessly. [7]But they had no child, because Elizabeth was barren and both were advanced in years. [8]Once when he was serving as priest in his division's turn before God, [9]according to the practice of the priestly service, he was chosen by lot to enter the sanctuary of the Lord to burn incense. [10]Then, when the whole assembly of the people was praying outside at the hour of the incense offering, [11]the angel of the Lord appeared to him, standing at the right of the altar of incense. [12]Zechariah was troubled by what he saw, and fear came upon him. [13]But the angel said to him, "Do not be afraid, Zechariah, because your prayer has been heard. Your wife Elizabeth will bear you a son, and you shall name him John. [14]And you will have joy and gladness, and many will rejoice at his birth, [15]for he will be great in the sight of [the] Lord. He will drink neither wine nor strong drink. He will be filled with the holy Spirit even from his mother's womb, [16]and he will turn many of the children of Israel to the Lord their God. [17]He will go before him in the spirit and power of Elijah to turn the hearts of fathers toward children and the disobedient to the understanding of the righteous, to prepare a people fit for the

33

Lord." [18]Then Zechariah said to the angel, "How shall I know this? For I am an old man, and my wife is advanced in years." [19]And the angel said to him in reply, "I am Gabriel, who stand before God. I was sent to speak to you and to announce to you this good news. [20]But now you will be speechless and unable to talk until the day these things take place, because you did not believe my words, which will be fulfilled at their proper time."

[21]Meanwhile the people were waiting for Zechariah and were amazed that he stayed so long in the sanctuary. [22]But when he came out, he was unable to speak to them, and they realized that he had seen a vision in the sanctuary. He was gesturing to them but remained mute. [23]Then, when his days of ministry were completed, he went home. [24]After this time his wife Elizabeth conceived, and she went into seclusion for five months, saying, [25]"So has the Lord done for me at a time when he has seen fit to take away my disgrace before others."

After an elegant preface in classical Greek style (vv. 1-4), Luke begins the infancy narrative with verse 5 using Jewish vocabulary and the semitic style of Israel's ancient Scriptures. The description of the central characters indicates that their relationship with the God of Israel is the dominant feature of their lives.

Zechariah was a priest, belonging to one of the twenty-four divisions of priests named for the twenty-four sons of the high priest Aaron. His wife Elizabeth was from the priestly family of Aaron, and she was named after the wife of Aaron. They were "righteous" before God, blamelessly following the law of God, personifying Jewish devotion at its best. Their faithful adherence to their ancient religion enabled them to be receptive to the new ways the God of their ancestors would act.

The childless state of the couple, their old age, and the infertility of Elizabeth present a situation of shame and human hopelessness about the future. In Israel's society children were an economic necessity and were the means of continuing the family line. Yet, throughout salvation history, God has used such conditions as the ground of new possibilities. The father and mother of Israel, Abraham and Sarah, were likewise in such a condition when God intervened at the dawn of salvific history.

The Gospel of Luke begins and ends in the Temple of Jerusalem. No place was more representative of the presence and promises of God. Zechariah's presence within the inner sanctuary, offering incense to

God at the time of prayer, indicates that God is working within the ritual symbols and institutions of Israel. The new era of salvation is heir to all that God has done already through the covenanted life of Israel.

It was a rare privilege to be chosen to offer incense in the Temple. Zechariah's priestly office led him into the sanctuary (the Holy Place, not the inner Holy of Holies) to scatter incense on the burning coals of the altar. This offering, commanded in Exodus 30:7-8, was accompanied by the prayers of the people of Israel who gathered outside.

The annunciation to Zechariah follows the pattern of birth announcements from the Old Testament. First, the angel (or God) appears; second, the recipient is troubled and fearful; third, reassurance is given and the birth is announced; fourth, the recipient raises an objection; and fifth, a confirming sign is given.

The appearance of the angel Gabriel reminds the reader of the same angel's appearance to Daniel (Dan 9:20–10:15). As in the manifestation to Zechariah, Gabriel appeared while Daniel was praying at the time of the evening sacrifice in the Temple. Daniel was afraid and was told not to fear, and, like Zechariah, he was struck speechless. The message to Daniel is a sweeping description of God's final plan—the coming of an anointed one, the ratification of prophecy, and the introduction of the everlasting justice of the messianic era. The reappearance of the angel here suggests that the time of fulfillment has arrived.

The angel proclaims that Elizabeth will have a son. Zechariah is to name him John, a name which means "Yahweh has shown favor," indicating the child's role in the ongoing drama of salvation. His birth is the answer to prayer, not only the personal prayer of Zechariah for a child but the hopeful prayer of Israel for salvation. "Joy and gladness," to be experienced by the parents as well as by many in Israel, is the response associated by the prophets with the messianic age.

Verses 15-17 anticipate the scope of John's future mission. First, John "will be great" in his dedication to God's work. Jesus will later testify: "Among those born of women, no one is greater than John" (7:28). Second, he will refrain from wine and strong drink, as in the Nazarite tradition (Num 6:3). Like Samson and Samuel he will be set apart for dedication to the Lord. Third, he will be "filled with the holy Spirit," the essential mark of a prophet in the Old Testament. Instead of strong drink, God's spirit will fill him. At Pentecost, the community who was thought to be drunk, had actually received the Holy Spirit and had begun to prophesy. Fourth, he will turn many in Israel to the Lord. This is Old Testament language for repentance, anticipating the prophetic ministry of John who will come "proclaiming a baptism of repentance for the forgiveness of sins" (3:3).

In describing John's role of preparing the people for the advent of Christ, the angel says: "He will go before him in the spirit and power of Elijah." Elijah was a prophetic reformer in Israel. The Jews expected him to return, heralding the advent of the Messiah, reconciling the people of Israel, and making the people ready for the Lord. In the last prophetic book of the Old Testament, Malachi proclaims: "Lo, I am sending my messenger to prepare the way before me . . . Lo, I will send you Elijah, the prophet, before the day of the LORD comes" (Mal 3:1, 23).

All that is said about John demonstrates that his mission is continuous with God's interventions throughout Israel's history. The old will usher in the new. His life will bring the entire prophetic history of Israel to a climax. He will be that voice crying in the wilderness "Prepare the way of the Lord" (3:4), preparing the people of ancient Israel to be the renewed people of God.

The presence of angels as messengers of God is frequent in the writings of the Old Testament, and their presence is abundant in the New Testament literature. The appearance of Gabriel, as the revelatory angel of Daniel, evokes a sense of Israel's expectations of deliverance and the glory of the days to come. He is one of three angels named in the Old Testament, along with Michael and Raphael, and in other Jewish literature he is listed as one of the seven angels of God's presence. Gabriel, here, as the messenger of God, is the first to proclaim the "good news." This announcement of the Gospel will be the mission of John, Jesus, and the apostles.

Zechariah reacted cautiously and doubtfully to Gabriel's proclamation. "How am I to know that?" echoes the objection of the incredulous Abraham to the divine revelation (Gen 15:8). Zechariah is concerned with human problems and wants a proof, while Gabriel focuses on the power of God. Zechariah's response contrasts with that of Mary who expresses wonder at the action of God.

Zechariah, because he has been struck mute, is unable to utter the good news. Apparently he has also been made deaf, since the people have to make signs to him (1:62). The silence of Zechariah serves several functions in the narrative: It creates a mood of mysterious expectation for what is to happen next, it allows Zechariah a time of quiet reflection on the wonders God is working, and it creates a strong contrast with the responses of Mary to the message of God's will.

The ordinary practice of the Temple priests was to conclude their duties in the sanctuary by going out to pronounce the priestly blessing (Num 6:24-26) over the assembled people. Unable to speak, Zechariah does not utter the blessing. This priestly blessing, unable to be given at the beginning of the Gospel, will be given at the Gospel's conclusion by the risen Christ. As he "raised his hands and blessed them" (24:50), Jesus is shown to be the ideal high priest.

The scene ends with Zechariah's return home and Elizabeth's conception. She, unlike Zechariah, immediately recognizes what the Lord has done for her, and she gives praise for the way God reverses human expectation. The humanly impossible becomes possible with God. This pregnant old woman and mute old man represent the possibilities within those who trust. Her barren womb will give birth to God's promise; his mute tongue will issue forth in praise.

Luke 1:26-38 Announcement of the Birth of Jesus

[26]In the sixth month, the angel Gabriel was sent from God to a town of Galilee called Nazareth, [27]to a virgin betrothed to a man named Joseph, of the house of David, and the virgin's name was Mary. [28]And coming to her, he said, "Hail, favored one! The Lord is with you." [29]But she was greatly troubled at what was said and pondered what sort of greeting this might be. [30]Then the angel said to her, "Do not be afraid, Mary, for you have found favor with God. [31]Behold, you will conceive in your womb and bear a son, and you shall name him Jesus. [32]He will be great and will be called Son of the Most High, and the Lord God will give him the throne of David his father, [33]and he will rule over the house of Jacob forever, and of his kingdom there will be no end." [34]But Mary said to the angel, "How can this be, since I have no relations with a man?" [35]And the angel said to her in reply, "The holy Spirit will come upon you, and the power of the Most High will overshadow you. Therefore the child to be born will be called holy, the Son of God. [36]And behold, Elizabeth, your relative, has also conceived a son in her old age, and this is the sixth month for her who was called barren; [37]for nothing will be impossible for God." [38]Mary said, "Behold, I am the handmaid of the Lord. May it be done to me according to your word." Then the angel departed from her.

Luke connects this scene and the previous annunciation by indicating that the same divine messenger appeared and that this scene occurred six months after the previous one. Likewise, the same five-fold pattern of Old Testament birth announcements is demonstrated here: angelic appearance, fear, announcement, objection, and sign. These parallels with the birth announcements of Ishmael, Isaac, Samson, Samuel, and John the Baptist emphasize the unity of God's plan. But the connections also serve to highlight more strikingly the significant contrasts.

The setting moves away from the priestly ambiance of the Temple in Jerusalem to a small town in Galilee. Nazareth was quite insignificant at the time and was never mentioned in the Scriptures of Israel. The situation of the central characters has also shifted. Zechariah and Elizabeth were elderly and barren, yet, like many other righteous ones in the Hebrew Scriptures, God overcame their human inability to conceive. God's intervention in the lives of Mary and Joseph, however, was unlike anything before in salvation history, as new as God's original creation.

This radical newness is emphasized by the double insistence in verse 27 that Mary is a virgin. God's intervention was not in response to her yearning for a child nor was it the result of anything she could have anticipated. Mary was betrothed to Joseph, but they had not come to live together. Whereas all of God's previous interventions to bring about the birth of a child presumed the cooperation of a human couple and sexual intercourse, Mary's conception is described as a divine creative action without the normal means of procreation.

The annunciation in Luke's account focuses on Mary as the recipient of God's revelation. Luke makes much less of Joseph's role throughout the infancy narrative than does Matthew. Yet Luke, like Matthew, insists on the Davidic lineage of Joseph, thus emphasizing the critical role of Joseph for Jesus' messianic identity. Luke's stress on Joseph's legal paternity and Mary's singular physical maternity is reemphasized in 3:23: "He was the son, as was thought, of Joseph." Luke indicates here that Jesus was not the natural son of Joseph, as many thought, but that he was Joseph's heir in the line of David.

The Greek word translated as "hail," a normal Greek greeting, can also be translated as "rejoice." The verb as used in the Greek Old Testament expresses joy over a manifestation of God's salvation. The word translated "favored one" is rooted in the Greek word for "grace, favor, blessing, or gift," especially as a manifestation of God's presence. Mary is blessed because God has chosen her for his salvific plan. This divine grace or favor is confirmed by the angel: "You have found favor with God." Her great favor is the grace of conceiving the Son of God.

"The Lord is with you" is a frequent expression throughout the Scriptures. It expressed God's assurances to Isaac, Jacob, Moses, Gideon, and Jeremiah in their divine callings. As it is used here and as a greeting in Christian liturgy, it is a pledge of God's protective and guiding presence. No matter what obstacles Mary faces, God's plans for her will be realized.

Mary was deeply disturbed and confused by what the angel said. But the angel responded to her shock with the frequent phrase from the Scriptures of Israel: "Do not be afraid." Gabriel then began the divine message with the standard form so well known from the Hebrew tradition: She will conceive in her womb, she will give birth to a son, and she will give him the divinely chosen name. However, the remainder of the angelic message, concerning the future accomplishments of the child, is far from standard.

Among the many Old Testament echoes found throughout the annunciation scene are passages associating Mary with Israel. If the opening word of the angelic announcement is urging Mary to "rejoice," Luke may have been evoking the messianic prophecy of Zephaniah 3:14-17 in the angelic greeting: "Rejoice, O daughter Zion . . . The King of Israel, the Lord, is in your midst . . . Fear not, O Zion . . . The Lord, your God, is in your midst, a mighty savior." "Daughter Zion" was a personification of Israel in the prophetic writings. Zephaniah announced that the joyful Zion would be filled with the presence of the Lord in the messianic age; Gabriel announced that the Lord would be with Mary and that she would give birth to the Savior.

In the Church's early preaching, the primary titles attributed to Jesus are "Messiah/Christ" and "Son of God." The infancy narratives are a proclamation of this Gospel message, announcing this twofold identity of Jesus to the world. The heart of the annunciation scene declares that the child to be born will be the Davidic Messiah (vv. 32-33) and the Son of God (v. 35). His advent is from Israel as David's heir and from God as the divine Son.

Gabriel describes the future greatness of the child in words that echo the prophecies concerning the Messiah. The foundational text for Israel's messianic hope is found in the promise Nathan delivered to David (2 Sam 7:12-16). God promised David that his heir would reign on his throne and that his kingdom would last forever. God also promised, "I will be a father to him, and he shall be a son to me" (2 Sam 7:14).

The angel announces that everything expected for the Davidic Messiah will be fulfilled in Jesus. "Most High" is a frequent title for God in the Old Testament and the Lukan writings. "Son of the Most High" is a messianic title here, yet Jesus will declare to his followers that those who love generously will be "sons of the Most High" (6:35). The Jewish hopes are echoed in the declarations that God will give Jesus the "throne of David his father," that "he will rule over the house of Jacob forever," and that "of his kingdom there will be no end."

The promise of an everlasting kingdom is also reflected in other prophetic texts. Isaiah announced that the son to be born would reign forever from David's throne (Isa 9:5-6). Daniel proclaims the coming of a messianic figure whose dominion is everlasting and whose kingship shall not be destroyed (Dan 7:14). The text of Amos is used in Acts to proclaim that the reign of Christ restores the fallen house of David (Amos 9:11; Acts 15:15).

This messianic identity of Jesus proclaimed at the annunciation will be developed throughout the writings of Luke. The royal psalms express Christ's divine sonship, "You are my son; today I am your father" (Ps 2:7), a theme developed at the baptism and transfiguration. Christ's fulfillment of the Davidic prophecies is especially illuminated by his resurrection. His reign at God's right hand, "The LORD said to you, my lord: `Take your throne at my right hand'" (Ps 110:1), is a theme developed in Acts.

Mary's puzzled response and her insistence that she has had no relations with a man accomplishes several purposes in the narrative. It confirms her virginity of which we were previously informed; it expresses wonder at this extraordinary announcement of something that is humanly impossible; and it moves the dialogue to the next stage of revelation about who this child will be. Mary's question makes clear that the plan of God would not be accomplished through a human begetting of the child; the angel's response explains that the child would be conceived through God's creative intervention.

Gabriel goes on to describe the extraordinary manner in which Mary will conceive and so reports the child's true origins. The "holy Spirit" and the "power of the Most High" are parallel expressions of God's creative power, made known in many ways through the history of Israel's salvation. Now, because of this wondrous action of God breaking forth into human history, the child to be born will be the "Son of God." This title of divine sonship means much more than the adoptive sonship which Davidic kings received at their coronation. Jesus will have a unique filial relationship to the God of Israel from his conception in Mary's womb. "The Most High," "the Son of God," and "the holy Spirit," described as the Trinity in later doctrine, are present here at this climactic moment of saving grace.

This twofold announcement of Jesus' identity, as "Messiah" and "Son of God," anticipates the twin questions at the trial of Jesus concerning his messiahship and his divine sonship (22:67, 70). It also anticipates the Church's earliest theology reflected in Paul's writings as he proclaims that Jesus is "descended from David according to the flesh, but established as Son of God in power" (Rom 1:3-4). Luke is indicating that the manifestations of Jesus' identity at his baptism, transfiguration, and resurrection are wider proclamations of the identity which Jesus already possessed from his conception.

While the primary focus of this angelic announcement is the child's identity, it also proclaims the dignity of his mother. The Spirit of God, which moved over the waters to bring creation from the abyss (Gen 1:2), comes upon Mary to bring forth the new creation from her virgin womb. The same Holy Spirit will come upon the disciples at Pentecost (Acts 1:8), creating the new people of Christ's Church.

At the end of the Book of Exodus, God fulfilled the divine promise and came to dwell in the midst of the people. The cloud of God's presence overshadowed the tabernacle in the desert and the glory of God filled it (Exod 40:35). Clearly the overshadowing of God's presence which fills the womb of Mary alludes to this fulfillment of God's promises among his ancient people. Mary thus becomes a tabernacle of God's presence dwelling with God's people.

The sign given to Mary that confirms the angel's announcement is the pregnancy of Elizabeth, her elderly kinswoman. The secret of the past five months is now made known. The angel concludes the annunciation by expressing the trusting confidence urged upon all who receive God's promises: "Nothing will be impossible for God." Israel's ancient ancestor Sarah had responded with a skeptical laugh when told that she would bear a son in her old age. The Lord responded to her: "Is anything too marvelous for the LORD to do?" (Gen 18:14). Mary, however, responds with a total, joyful acceptance of God's great gift. Jesus will teach his disciples the same wisdom when speaking

41

about the importance of trusting God as the source of all saving grace: "What is impossible for human beings is possible for God" (18:27).

Mary's response, "May it be done to me according to your word," flows from her trusting faith and humble obedience to God's will. Mary received the Word of God in her heart, and thus consented to conceive the Son of God in her womb. As the first to hear the Gospel of Jesus Christ, she is an ideal disciple because she is a woman of the "word."

Her receptivity to the Word of God looks ahead to her discipleship throughout the Gospel and into the early Church. She receives God's Word, reflects on it in her heart, and commits her life to it. As the model disciple, she is first among the true family of disciples, "those who hear the word of God and act on it" (8:21). Mary cooperates with God's saving plan as faithfully as her Son who would say at the end of his life, "Not my will but yours be done" (22:42).

Luke 1:39-45 Mary Visits Elizabeth

> [39]During those days Mary set out and traveled to the hill country in haste to a town of Judah, [40]where she entered the house of Zechariah and greeted Elizabeth. [41]When Elizabeth heard Mary's greeting, the infant leaped in her womb, and Elizabeth, filled with the holy Spirit, [42]cried out in a loud voice and said, "Most blessed are you among women, and blessed is the fruit of your womb. [43]And how does this happen to me, that the mother of my Lord should come to me? [44]For at the moment the sound of your greeting reached my ears, the infant in my womb leaped for joy. [45]Blessed are you who believed that what was spoken to you by the Lord would be fulfilled."

The meeting of Elizabeth and Mary brings together the two parallel annunciations and prepares for the two parallel birth scenes. The two women represent the meeting of the old covenant and the new covenant. One is elderly and will have a son who will be the last great figure of ancient Israel; the other is young and will have a son who will usher in the new age of salvation. Their joyful unity expresses the harmony between the traditional faith of Israel and the advent of the Savior.

In Mary the new covenant reaches out to the old covenant, giving it ultimate meaning and preparing for its fulfillment. In Elizabeth the old covenant recognizes the new and gives honor to its coming.

The prophetic action of John in the womb prepares for the relationship between John and Jesus in adulthood. Ancient Israel and the reign of God intersect: "The law and the prophets lasted until John; but from then on the kingdom of God is proclaimed" (16:16).

Mary, having received a revelation of what God had done for Elizabeth, traveled in haste to greet her relative. Elizabeth, her seclusion at an end with Mary's greeting, receives a revelation of what God had done for Mary. The revelation comes through the movement of the unborn John, already prophesying and acclaiming the coming of the Lord.

The Holy Spirit is active within those who prophesy about the significance of the Lord's coming. John's prophetic leap begins to fulfill the angel's revelation, "He will be filled with the holy Spirit even from his mother's womb" (1:15). Elizabeth too is "filled with the holy Spirit" as she sings in praise of God's work in Mary. Zechariah and Simeon too will be filled with the Holy Spirit and burst forth in prophetic praise, anticipating the prophetic utterances unleashed by the Holy Spirit at Pentecost.

Elizabeth proclaims, "Most blessed are you among women." God has exalted Mary among all the women of Israel: Sarah, Rachel, Hannah, Deborah, Jael (Judg 5:24), and Judith (Jdt 13:18); for Mary has been chosen to bring to birth the hope of all the ages. The women of Israel had been instruments of God's saving will, either by bringing forth new hope through their children or by delivering the people from their enemies. "Blessed be the fruit of your womb" is the blessing God promised in the Torah (Deut 28:4) to those who harkened to the voice of God.

Elizabeth's question, "And how does this happen to me, that the mother of my Lord should come to me," echoes the question of David when he feared God's presence in the Ark of the Covenant: "How can the ark of the LORD come to me?" (2 Sam 6:9). The link between Mary and the ark of the covenant is suggested by the fact that the ark bore the divine presence just as Mary carried the Lord in her womb. The link is further suggested by remembering that the ark remained in the house of Odededom for three months and the Lord blessed his house (2 Sam 6:11) in the hill country of Judah. Likewise, Mary stayed in the house of Zechariah for three months and the home was blessed with the Lord's presence.

"Mother of my Lord" implies that Jesus is the royal Messiah and that Mary is the king's mother. Luke reflects, as does Matthew, the central role of the king's mother in the birth, enthronement, and reign of the Davidic kings of Judah. "My Lord" refers to the words of David (Ps 110:1), used in the writings of Luke to suggest that the Messiah is both David's son and David's Lord (20:42-44). The same royal psalm is quoted in Peter's speech at Pentecost, proclaiming that in the resurrection, "God has made him (Jesus) both Lord and Messiah" (Acts 2:36).

Throughout Luke's Gospel, God is referred to as "Lord." This follows the Greek Old Testament where *Yahweh* is translated as "Lord." Reflecting the faith of the early Church which acclaimed that "Jesus is Lord," Luke's writings refer to Jesus throughout as "Lord." It is the highest title of Jesus, associated particularly with his resurrection (24:34) and exaltation and implying in some sense that he is on a level with Yahweh. In calling Mary "mother" of the Lord, Luke proclaims that Jesus was Lord from the beginnings of his existence in the womb of Mary. Because she conceived and gave flesh to the one who would be enthroned in heaven (Acts 2:33), she remains the mother of the Lord forever.

The words of Elizabeth proclaim that Mary is most blessed because she bears the Lord in her womb (vv. 42-43) and because she has believed the Word of God: "Blessed are you who believed that what was spoken to you by the Lord would be fulfilled" (v. 45). Thus Mary is praised both as the Mother of the Lord and as the model for Christian believers. This anticipates the beatitude pronounced by a woman in the crowd during Jesus' public ministry about how wonderful a mother such a gifted son must have: "Blessed is the womb that carried you and the breasts at which you nursed." Jesus agrees that his mother is worthy of praise, not just because she gave him birth, but because she is among those who have believed God's Word: "Rather, blessed are those who hear the Word of God and observe it" (11:27-28).

Mary is the ideal disciple because she is committed to God's Word; she is a hearer of the Word and a doer of the Word. After receiving the Gospel, she hastens to share that Word with another in need. She surrenders herself to God's plan; she is full of gratitude for the gifts she receives; she has a contemplative sense of wonder at the mysteries of God.

Luke 1:46-56 The Canticle of Mary

⁴⁶And Mary said:
"My soul proclaims the greatness of the Lord;
⁴⁷ my spirit rejoices in God my savior.
⁴⁸For he has looked upon his handmaid's lowliness;
  behold, from now on will all ages call me blessed.
⁴⁹The Mighty One has done great things for me,
  and holy is his name.
⁵⁰His mercy is from age to age
  to those who fear him.
⁵¹He has shown might with his arm,
  dispersed the arrogant of mind and heart.
⁵²He has thrown down the rulers from their thrones
  but lifted up the lowly.
⁵³The hungry he has filled with good things;
  the rich he has sent away empty.
⁵⁴He has helped Israel his servant,
  remembering his mercy,
⁵⁵according to his promise to our fathers,
  to Abraham and to his descendants forever."
⁵⁶Mary remained with her about three months and then returned to her home.

Luke's infancy narrative contains four hymns, traditionally named by the opening words in their Latin translation: the *Magnificat* (1:46-55), the *Benedictus* (1:68-79), the *Gloria* (2:14), and the *Nunc Dimittis* (2:29-32). These songs were probably sung within the Jewish Christian community before the Gospel was written, and they were inserted by Luke into his writing rather than being composed by him.

The songs are mosaics pieced together from many Old Testament passages, quite similar in style to the psalms. They demonstrate how rooted the early Christians were in the ancient expressions of Israel's faith, and they also express a deep sense that salvation has been accomplished through fulfillment of God's promises to Abraham and David. They express the Jewish faith of the early Church as well as the faith of the character who sings the song as a representative of the messianic community.

In her canticle Mary gives praise for all that God has done for her. Because of her humility she is able to experience joy and gratitude for God's bounteous favors. Her praise for what God has personally done for her widens to include what God has done for everyone in

45

every age, especially what God is doing for Israel in bringing forth the Messiah. Mary is again depicted as the representative of Israel, the embodiment of the people of God. The mercy that God has shown to Mary exemplifies the mercy God shows to his people.

Since Mary is a woman of the Word of God, she would have been quite familiar with the many passages from the Scriptures of Israel that echo throughout her canticle. The psalms, the daily prayers of the Jewish people, most influence the song. Mary is part of a long line of women who sing songs of praise in the Old Testament: Miriam (Exod 15:20-21), Deborah (Judg 5), Hannah (1 Sam 2:1-10), and Judith (Jdt 16:1-17).

Mary's response most resembles that of Hannah. When told that God would grant her prayers for a son, Hannah expresses her lowliness before God and calls herself God's "handmaid." The song of Mary is modeled on the song of Hannah. Both women praise God for choosing them as instruments of God's saving intervention in Israel's history. Hannah rejoices in the favors God has shown to her: "My heart exults in the LORD" (1 Sam 2:1). She praises God for reversing the conditions of the proud and mighty and raising up the needy and the poor.

Mary recognizes God as her "savior." The title here is used of Yahweh, but in 2:11 it will be given to Jesus. What God is doing through her will bring about a new age of salvation. Throughout Luke's writings, salvation is central. Through the coming of the Savior, God's people are delivered from evil and alienation and they are restored to right relations with God. Mary rejoices in the salvation that God will bring through the life of her son.

Verse 48 seems to refer most directly to Mary herself. Her "lowliness" refers to her unworthiness to be the mother of the Messiah as well as the objective poverty and powerlessness of her position. She calls herself God's "handmaid," the feminine form of "servant," which connects her song with her response to the annunciation (v. 38). "From now on will all ages call me blessed" refers to the attitude of future generations of believers toward her who will bear the Savior.

Verses 49-50 contrast Mary's humble lowliness with God's greatness. The "great things" refers in the Old Testament to God's wonderful accomplishments made known in the Exodus (Deut 10:21). Now the God of the ancient covenant is again doing great things for Mary and her people. Mary sings of God's primary attributes: mightiness, holiness, and mercy. Yahweh is the "Mighty One" who cares for the lowly and the "Holy One" who chooses to dwell among his people. God's endless "mercy" refers to Yahweh's covenant love in which God chose Israel without any merit on the people's part. The advent of the Savior is a new expression of God's might, holiness, and mercy made known from of old.

Verses 51-53 sing of God's great deeds. The praises offered to God for what he has done also announce what God will continue to do. The strength of God's "arm" expresses God's redeeming power throughout Israel's history. God reverses the conditions that human beings have created. God exalts the lowly and needy, putting down the proud, powerful, and wealthy. This pattern of complete reversal of fortunes will be evident throughout the Gospel. In Jesus' sermon on the plain, he proclaims that the poor, hungry, weeping, and hated are blessed because their condition will be reversed (6:20-26). In his parable of the rich man and Lazarus, the poor beggar is blessed in the end. This unexpected reversal, which is most fully expressed in the cross of Christ, is already manifested in God's choice of Mary.

As her song concludes (vv. 54-55), Mary places herself within the long line of promises made to Abraham and his descendants. God had promised that all nations of the earth would be blessed through the descendants of Abraham. What God has done for this daughter of Abraham is set within the context of God's total plan for Israel. God's promise of blessing is being fulfilled as Mary, like Sarah before her, gives birth to the promised one of God. The salvation to be made known through the birth, ministry, death, and resurrection of Jesus fulfills the covenant God had made with the ancestors of Israel.

Luke 1:57-66 The Birth of John

[57]When the time arrived for Elizabeth to have her child she gave birth to a son. [58]Her neighbors and relatives heard that the Lord had shown his great mercy toward her, and they rejoiced with her. [59]When they came on the eighth day to circumcise the child, they were going to call him Zechariah after his father, [60]but his mother said in reply, "No. He will be called John." [61]But they answered her, "There is no one among your relatives who has this name." [62]So they made signs, asking his father what he wished him to be called. [63]He asked for a tablet and wrote, "John is his name," and all were amazed. [64]Immediately his mouth was opened, his tongue freed, and he spoke blessing God. [65]Then fear came upon all their neighbors, and all these matters were

discussed throughout the hill country of Judea. [66]All who heard these things took them to heart, saying, "What, then, will this child be?" For surely the hand of the Lord was with him.

The birth, circumcision, naming, and manifestation of John evoke the atmosphere of the Old Testament, emphasizing his roots in the covenant with Israel. Like Abraham and Sarah of old, the elderly Zechariah and Elizabeth have a son in fulfillment of God's promises. Like their ancestors, they name their son and circumcise him on the eighth day after his birth. As all who heard of the birth of Sarah's son rejoiced with her, all who heard of the birth of Elizabeth's son rejoiced with her (Gen 21:1-6). The scene also prepares the way for the birth, circumcision, naming, and manifestation of Jesus.

The Torah instructed that all the sons of Israel be circumcised when they are eight days old. God had commanded Abraham to institute circumcision as a sign of the covenant for all his descendants (Gen 17:10-14). It marked those who belonged to the chosen people and was a reminder to both God and the Israelites that they were to share in the responsibilities and blessings of the covenant.

The name John means "Yahweh has shown favor." The repetition of the name emphasizes the divine favor, and the uniqueness of the name in the family's history points to the extraordinary significance of his life. The name speaks of his origin and his future; he comes as a divine favor to Elizabeth and he will manifest God's favor upon all Israel.

Zechariah named his son according to the command of the angel, reversing his earlier reluctance to believe and accept God's Word (1:20). Because he opened his heart, God opened his mouth. Zechariah's response now matches that of Mary and Elizabeth. As he obeys God's Word he is freed to give praise to God.

This charming scene in the hill country becomes filled with fear and wonder as people of the village become aware of the presence of God in the events unfolding before them. The manifestation of John to the relatives and neighbors and then to the entire hill country of Judea hints at his eventual manifestation to all Israel. All who heard of these matters pondered their significance and asked: "What, then, will this child be?" The answer begins to be heard in the canticle that follows, but the complete response will come in the future. The question establishes a sense of anticipation for the future unfolding of God's plan in the public ministry of John the Baptist.

Luke 1:67-80 The Canticle of Zechariah

[67]Then Zechariah his father, filled with the holy Spirit, prophesied, saying:
[68]"Blessed be the Lord, the God of Israel,
  for he has visited and brought redemption to his people.
[69]He has raised up a horn for our salvation
  within the house of David his servant,
[70]even as he promised through the mouth of his holy
    prophets from of old:
[71] salvation from our enemies and from the hand of all who
    hate us,
[72]to show mercy to our fathers
  and to be mindful of his holy covenant
[73]and of the oath he swore to Abraham our father,
  and to grant us that, [74]rescued from the hand of enemies,
    without fear we might worship him [75]in holiness and right-
    eousness
  before him all our days.
[76]And you, child, will be called prophet of the Most High,
  for you will go before the Lord to prepare his ways,
[77]to give his people knowledge of salvation
  through the forgiveness of their sins,
[78]because of the tender mercy of our God
  by which the daybreak from on high will visit us
[79]to shine on those who sit in darkness and death's shadow,
  to guide our feet into the path of peace."
[80]The child grew and became strong in spirit, and he was in the
desert until the day of his manifestation to Israel.

The canticle of Zechariah praises God for fulfilling the ancient
promises by sending the Savior. The Jewish Christians who sang
this hymn before its incorporation into Luke's Gospel expressed
their faith entirely within the context of the tradition of Israel. The
advent of salvation is described with the language and imagery of
the Old Testament, yet the hymn is filled with the radiance of the
Savior's dawning.

The song expresses Zechariah's praise of God after his mouth was
opened and his tongue was freed. He is described as "filled with the
holy Spirit" and uttering prophecy. Because Elizabeth had been
filled with the Holy Spirit (v. 41), she was able to recognize the true
significance of Mary in God's plan. Because Zechariah was filled
with the Holy Spirit, he was able to recognize the significance of

John in the plan of God. Both Mary and John play crucial roles in this time of Christ's advent.

The opening line of the song, "Blessed be the Lord, the God of Israel," is a common beginning for Jewish blessing prayers, taken from the psalms (Pss 41:14; 72:18; 106:48). The prayer was also uttered by David when his son Solomon succeeded him on the throne of Israel (1 Kgs 1:48). God's promise to David's line, begun to be answered in his successors, is fulfilled in Jesus the Messiah.

God "visited" his people, a Hebrew description of God's historical interventions, by raising up a "horn for our salvation." The "saving horn" is an image derived from the action of a wild animal tossing its horn in a display of power. The image described God's saving strength in Psalm 18:3 and is used here as a title for the Messiah. The end of Hannah's song (1 Sam 2:10) prays for the strength of the king, "the horn of God's anointed." The image refers to the Davidic king as an instrument of God's salvation (Ps 132:17; Ezek 29:21) and thus becomes a messianic title.

This definitive time of salvation is described as the fulfillment of God's promises to Israel's ancient ancestors. The hopes of Israel are fulfilled as God keeps his promises to David (2 Sam 7:12-16) and his oath to Abraham (Gen 22:16-18). Recall how the beginning of Matthew's Gospel describes Jesus as son of David and son of Abraham. Both Zechariah's canticle and Matthew's genealogy express the theme of God's preparation for salvation through David and Abraham.

The covenant established through Abraham, Moses, and David is the foundation of God's relationship with his people and the root of all God's promises. God expresses the covenant through his loving kindness (ḥesed), which is here translated "mercy" (v. 73). God's people express the covenant through "worship" of God (v. 74), a worship expressed through the covenant virtues of "holiness and righteousness" (v. 75). The proper response to God's constant fidelity is a way of living that can be described as worship of God, a life marked by holy living and faithful observance of the covenant. Luke will show how this covenant fidelity, exemplified in the lives of Mary, Elizabeth, and Zechariah, is expressed by the Church, described in Acts as a worshipping community.

Verse 76 begins the second part of the canticle in which Zechariah sings of the prophetic mission of his newborn son and of John's relationship to the saving mission of Jesus. Jesus will be called "Son of the Most High" (1:32); John will be called "prophet of the Most High." John will be the last of the great prophets of Israel. He will be the herald and precursor, preparing people for the advent of salvation.

"You will go before the Lord to prepare his ways" expresses John's preparatory role, making clear that salvation is not from John but from the Lord. The term "Lord" here is deliberately ambiguous. The prophecy reflects the words of Isaiah: "Prepare the way of the LORD" (Isa 40:3; Mal 3:1). The Lord is the God of Israel, but the Lord is also Jesus, as Elizabeth already acknowledged by referring to Mary as mother of the Lord. The "way" John will make ready is the new way of salvation to be manifested in Jesus.

The prophetic words look ahead to the adult ministry of John. He will prepare the way by giving people "knowledge of salvation through the forgiveness of their sins." John will unveil Israel's salvation with his ritual washing and his preaching of repentance from sin (3:3f.). By giving people a foretaste, he prepares them to accept the full salvation and forgiveness that God wishes for all people.

The final image of the canticle referring to the advent of Christ is "the daybreak from on high" (v. 78). "Daybreak" may also be translated as "rising" (as a star or the sun) or "dawn." It was a term used by Jews to describe the expected Messiah, the shoot of David. Malachi prophesied that "there will arise the sun of justice with its healing rays" (Mal 3:20). We have seen how a "star at its rising" described the Messiah's birth in Matthew's infancy account (2:2).

The rising light shines so that people can share in the divine splendor. It illuminates those who are in darkness and those who need guidance (v. 79). The age of salvation is described in Isaiah as a glorious effulgence: "Rise up in splendor! Your light has come, the glory of the Lord shines upon you. See, darkness covers the earth . . . But upon you the LORD shines" (Isa 60:1-2).

This radiant image illumines the whole Gospel. The rising light guides our feet into "the path of peace." This shalom (peace) is the hope of Israel and a primary effect of the coming of Christ as it is expressed in Luke's writings. Such peace is not merely the absence of conflict; it is rather a state of complete wholeness and well-being that comes from God. It is the first greeting of the risen Lord to his disciples: "Peace be with you" (24:36). In Acts, Peter preached that God "proclaimed peace through Jesus Christ, who is Lord of all" (Acts 10:36).

The parallels between John and Jesus in the Gospel of Luke express what the fourth Gospel explicitly states about John: "He was not the light, but came to bear witness to the light" (John 1:8). The ministry of John will lead people to the light, the One who will shine on those in darkness. Verse 80 summarizes John's growth from infancy to manhood and anticipates his public mission. The word of God proclaimed in the infancy accounts will continue to be proclaimed: "The word of God came to John, son of Zechariah in the desert . . . ." (3:2).

The "desert" refers to the Judean wilderness, a barren steppe east of Jerusalem descending to the Jordan River. It is an environment similar to the desert of Sinai in which Israel prepared for the fulfillment of the covenant promises. In the wilderness are caves for shelter, basic vegetation, oases, locusts, and bees that produce wild honey. There is a credible theory that John spent his young years living in the community of Qumran, along the northwest shores of the Dead Sea.

The story of John's infancy is now complete. With verse 80 Luke has formed a bridge which connects the infancy of John to the day of his "manifestation to Israel." Full attention will now be given in chapter 2 to the dawning light, the birth of the Savior.

Luke 2:1-7 The Birth of Jesus

[1]In those days a decree went out from Caesar Augustus that the whole world should be enrolled. [2]This was the first enrollment, when Quirinius was governor of Syria. [3]So all went to be enrolled, each to his own town. [4]And Joseph too went up from Galilee from the town of Nazareth to Judea, to the city of David that is called Bethlehem, because he was of the house and family of David, [5]to be enrolled with Mary, his betrothed, who was with child. [6]While they were there, the time came for her to have her child, [7]and she gave birth to her firstborn son. She wrapped him in swaddling clothes and laid him in a manger, because there was no room for them in the inn.

Luke emphasizes the universal significance of the Savior's birth by the introduction of the world's emperor and the notice that "the whole world should be enrolled." In Luke's account of the Church's birth in Acts, he lists the peoples of the world and describes the gathering of people "from every nation under heaven" (Acts 2:5-11).

At the birth of Christ, the journey of everyone, each to his own town, for the universal enrollment anticipates the worldwide salvation that he will accomplish.

Jesus is born on a journey. The decree issued from Rome sets the world on a journey. When the Church is born, the Holy Spirit sets the Church on a journey "to the ends of the earth" (Acts 1:8). The Church's destiny is symbolized by the final journey of Paul to the city of Rome (Acts 28:14f). The decree of the Roman emperor at the time of Jesus' nativity looks forward to the expansion and the universal extent of Christ's saving work through the Church.

Caesar Augustus ruled the world. He was acknowledged as divine and proclaimed as "savior of the whole world," the one who brought "good news" to all. He was most recognized for the peace he established throughout the world during his reign. In the Gospel, Caesar Augustus is unknowingly an instrument in the saving plan of God. His decree brought the parents of Jesus to the town of Bethlehem for the birth of the true Savior, the one who brings real peace to the world. The political world proclaimed the peace of Augustus by building an altar in Rome, the Ara Pacis Augustus; the heavenly multitude proclaimed the peace of Christ by singing the good news of the Savior's birth in the city of David.

The census explains how Jesus of Nazareth is also Jesus of Bethlehem. Joseph traveled with Mary from Nazareth in Galilee to his ancestral town of Bethlehem in Judea. Bethlehem is the place of King David's origins and of his royal anointing (1 Sam 16). The birth of Jesus in Bethlehem is important for understanding his messianic identity. Because Joseph was of the lineage of David, his family belongs to the royal house of David.

The simplicity and lowly circumstances of Jesus' nativity contrast with the magnificent pageantry of the imperial court. The one promised by God entered history as a tiny, vulnerable creature. The Messiah's humble beginnings anticipate the stark contrasts between the pastoral authority of his disciples and the political dominion exercised by leaders of the world (22:24-27). The plain austerity of the birth in the midst of an expectant world veils the singular importance of this event for human history.

The description of Jesus as Mary's "firstborn son" is no indication that Mary had other children. It means, rather, that Jesus was to have the authority and status associated with the firstborn according to the Torah. The firstborn was to be consecrated to God (Exod 13:2;

Num 3:13), redeemed (Exod 13:13; Num 18:15), and receive the rights of inheritance (Deut 21:17).

The firstborn of Mary is also proclaimed in the Scriptures as the firstborn of God, as Israel was described as God's firstborn in the Old Testament (Exod 4:22). The messianic king, the heir to David's throne, was proclaimed as God's "firstborn" (Ps 89:28). Jesus is called the "firstborn of all creation" (Col 1:15) and the "firstborn of the dead" (Rev 1:5). In Hebrews it is said that the "angels of God worship him" when God "leads the first-born into the world" (Heb 1:6). The future children of Mary would be all those who follow Jesus since he is the "firstborn among many brothers" (Rom 8:29). Thus, this title for Jesus, which has such a rich history in ancient Israel, expresses his identity and mission in relationship to Israel's history, to all of creation, to his birth and resurrection, and to all who are born again as his brothers and sisters.

The maternal care of Mary for her newborn is demonstrated by the wrapping in "swaddling clothes." The bands of cloth which wrapped the child kept him warm and protected. Failure to swathe a newborn would be understood as a sign of neglect (Ezek 16:4). The description of Solomon's royal birth in the Book of Wisdom emphasizes his common humanity; he is formed in his mother's womb, wails as he is born, and is cared for with "swaddling clothes" (Wis 7:1-5). Like this first heir of David's throne, Jesus is born a royal son yet also shares the lot of all humanity.

The text does not state precisely the location in Bethlehem where Jesus was born. Since there was no place in the lodging for travelers, Mary and Joseph withdrew to a place where animals were kept, perhaps underneath or at the back of a house. An early tradition says the place of Jesus' birth was a cave, a natural place for keeping animals and their feed.

While vague about the location, Luke is quite interested in telling us where Mary laid the baby. The manger is a trough for feeding animals. In an area where wood was scarce, the manger was probably a low, hollow cavity in a rock ledge. The context suggests that the manger served as a cradle for the newborn. He who will be nourishment for the world, now lies in a manger because there was no place for him to lodge.

The manger is vitally important for Luke because it evokes the words of Isaiah: "An ox knows its owner, and an ass, its master's manger; but Israel does not know, my people has not understood"

(Isa 1:3). The Isaian passage is the reason for the introduction of oxen and donkeys into the traditional Christmas crèche. But more importantly, the passage in the context of Luke's account suggests that God's people have now begun to know their master's manger. In fact, the shepherds will find their Lord's manger and will glorify God.

Mary's care for Jesus at his birth, foreshadows the care shown for Jesus at his death. As Mary wrapped Jesus in cloths and laid him in the hollow rock of the manger, Joseph of Arimathea wrapped the body of Jesus in a linen cloth and laid him in a rock-hewn tomb (23:53). As Solomon had declared: "One is the entry into life for all; and in one same way they leave it" (Wis 7:6). The angel proclaimed that this infant wrapped in cloth and lying in a manger was a sign of the good news (2:12); the empty tomb with the burial cloths by themselves became a sign of the good news proclaimed by the angels at Christ's resurrection. Neither the cave of his birth nor the cave of his death gave rest to this transient traveler. This pilgrim who had "nowhere to rest his head" (9:58) was born on a journey and died on a journey.

Luke 2:8-14 Announcement to the Shepherds

8Now there were shepherds in that region living in the fields and keeping the night watch over their flock. 9The angel of the Lord appeared to them and the glory of the Lord shone around them, and they were struck with great fear. 10The angel said to them, "Do not be afraid; for behold, I proclaim to you good news of great joy that will be for all the people. 11For today in the city of David a savior has been born for you who is Messiah and Lord. 12And this will be a sign for you: you will find an infant wrapped in swaddling clothes and lying in a manger." 13And suddenly there was a multitude of the heavenly host with the angel, praising God and saying:
14"Glory to God in the highest
and on earth peace to those on whom his favor rests."

Because the shepherds are closely associated with Bethlehem, they evoke strong associations with David, the shepherd king. When David was tending his flock near the town of Bethlehem, he was chosen as king and anointed (1 Sam 16:11). God said to David, "You shall shepherd my people Israel" (2 Sam 5:2). The prophetic passage most responsible for the expectation that the Messiah would come from Bethlehem, Micah 5:1-3, also proclaims that he would "shepherd his flock."

Shepherds at the time of Jesus were people of low esteem. They were poor transients, often looked upon with suspicion by others, holding no social or religious status among the people of Israel. That they would be chosen as the first to hear the "good news of great joy" is surely an indication that God has "lifted up the lowly" (1:52). Jesus' birth among the poor anticipates his ministry to the poor and outcasts of Israel's society.

The simplicity of this pastoral scene in the quiet of the night contrasts with the extraordinary significance of Christ's birth. The rest of the world continues to go about its business while God's glory shines on a few shepherds in the field. During the night the shepherds would watch their flocks in shifts. This Lukan passage, along with Wisdom 18:14-15, "For when peaceful stillness compassed everything and the night in its swift course was half spent, Your all-powerful word from heaven's royal throne bounded," led to the tradition that Jesus was born at midnight.

The announcement of Christ's birth follows the pattern of other birth announcements. The angel appears to the shepherds, and they are struck with great fear. They are instructed not to be afraid, and the message is given. However, unlike other announcements, there is no objection given by the shepherds. Finally, a sign is given before the angel departs.

The announcement to the shepherds is described with the Greek verb *euangelizesthai*, "to proclaim the gospel/good news." This is a favorite verb for Luke, occurring frequently in both the Gospel and Acts. This proclamation of good news to the shepherds echoes the announcements in Isaiah: the anointed one is sent to proclaim good news to the lowly (Isa 61:1), the good news of peace and salvation (Isa 52:7). This "evangelization" to the shepherds anticipates the evangelizing mission given to the disciples of Jesus.

The joyful message of the angel announces that the one born in Bethlehem is Savior, Messiah, and Lord. This is the basic message of the infancy narrative, indeed, of the whole Gospel. "Savior" is the most significant title for Jesus in Luke's writings. As Savior, Jesus will rescue humanity from sin and heal the divisions that separate people from God and one another. As "Messiah," Jesus is the anointed heir of David, the one who will establish God's Kingdom. "Lord" is the most exalted expression of Jesus' identity. Used of both Yahweh and Jesus, the title points to his divine authority and transcendence.

These three titles proclaim the identity of Jesus which the disciples only fully understood after his resurrection. In Acts these titles reflect their earliest function as elements of the apostles' preaching (Acts 2:36; 5:31). In Paul's Letter to the Philippians these three titles refer to the expected return of Jesus: "Our citizenship is in heaven, and from it we also await a savior, the Lord Jesus Christ" (Phil 3:20). The interpretation of Jesus' birth comes to its climax as the angel affirms that Jesus was truly Savior, Christ, and Lord from the beginning.

In Isaiah 9:5-6 the prophet proclaims a message which brings great joy for the people: "A child is born to us, a son is given us. . . ." The newborn child is the heir to the throne of David, the anointed Immanuel of Isaiah 7–11. He is given royal titles, reflecting the attributes for which he will be known during his reign, a reign that will be "forever peaceful." This Isaian birth announcement becomes a model for Luke's proclamation of the newborn Savior.

The "sign" confirms the announcement. It is not the type of wondrous sign one might expect to announce the birth of the long-awaited Messiah of Israel. The humble simplicity of the sign, a baby swaddled in cloth and lying in a manger, is a strong contrast with the identity of the child which was just proclaimed. His poverty and his sovereignty invite the reader to ponder the mystery of this humble Savior, who will call the lowly to himself.

The angel is joined by a throng of the heavenly chorus praising God at the announcement of Christ's birth. The canticle of the angels, the Gloria, may have been a refrain sung by the early disciples in worship. It proclaims that heaven has touched earth in this wondrous birth. God in heaven is given glory; people on earth are brought peace.

The "peace" on earth proclaimed by the angels is the harmony and wholeness that only God can give. It is far greater than the mere absence of war brought by the peace of Emperor Augustus. One of the titles given to the Messiah in the Isaian birth announcement is "Prince of Peace" (Isa 9:5). In proclaiming the child to be born in Bethlehem, Micah announced: "He shall be peace" (Mic 5:4). Zechariah heralded the humble king-savior as he declared: "He shall proclaim peace to the nations" (Zech 9:10). The hope of Israel is fulfilled in Jesus through whom God brings "peace to those on whom his favor rests."

The canticle of the angels is closely paralleled by the canticle sung by the disciples as Jesus entered Jerusalem hailed as the messianic king: "Peace in heaven and glory in the highest" (19:38). Jesus is proclaimed as the peacemaker of God both at the beginning of his life and at the end. The angels recognize at his birth what the disciples came to understand at the end of his ministry. The "multitude of the heavenly host" proclaims peace on earth; the "multitude of his disciples" (19:37) on earth proclaims peace in heaven.

The good news of joy and peace announced by the angels anticipates the good news that will unfold throughout the narrative of Jesus' life, death, and resurrection. The shepherds and the angels prefigure the Church of Acts, a community that both receives the Gospel with humility and proclaims the Gospel with joy.

Luke 2:15-20 The Visit of the Shepherds

¹⁵When the angels went away from them to heaven, the shepherds said to one another, "Let us go, then, to Bethlehem to see this thing that has taken place, which the Lord has made known to us." ¹⁶So they went in haste and found Mary and Joseph, and the infant lying in the manger. ¹⁷When they saw this, they made known the message that had been told them about this child. ¹⁸All who heard it were amazed by what had been told them by the shepherds. ¹⁹And Mary kept all these things, reflecting on them in her heart. ²⁰Then the shepherds returned, glorifying and praising God for all they had heard and seen, just as it had been told to them.

In Matthew's account the birth of Jesus is manifested by a star to the magi; in Luke's account the birth is manifested by an angel to the shepherds. The magi of Matthew and the shepherds of Luke come to Bethlehem; they believe and worship, and then return from where they came. They represent the people to whom the good news will eventually be manifested—the Gentiles of the nations and the lowly of the earth.

Luke presents three different reactions to the angelic manifestation of the Savior's birth: the response of the shepherds (vv. 15-17, 20), those to whom the shepherds told the news (v. 18), and Mary (v. 19). Each of these demonstrates a response to the Gospel which Luke wishes the Christian reader to consider.

The shepherds trusted the divine message they had received and "went in haste" to see what they had been told. Their haste demonstrates the joyful energy which the Gospel generates in people. They see the "sign" and recognize their Lord in the manger (Isa 1:3). They "made known" to others what God had made known to them. They glorified and praised God for "all they had heard and seen." Their spontaneous trust in God's Word, their eager desire to make known the message, and their zeal to praise God for what they had seen and heard demonstrate the qualities of Christian discipleship. Their zeal anticipates that of Peter and John in Acts who said, "It is impossible for us not to speak about what we have seen and heard" (Acts 4:20).

The response of all those to whom the shepherds told the news (v. 18) and the response of Mary (v. 19) are contrasted. All who heard the message from the shepherds were "amazed by what they had been told." Amazement at the words and deeds of Jesus and his disciples is a common reaction throughout the Gospel and Acts. Yet, it is a superficial response that does not necessarily lead to faith. Mary, on the other hand, "kept all these things, reflecting on them in her heart."

These responses prefigure the many ways people will respond during the ministry of Jesus. Those who were amazed at what they were told are like those who will "receive the word with joy, but they have no root" (8:13). Mary is like those who will hear the word and "embrace it with a generous and good heart" (8:15). Though she is unable to understand the meaning of all the words she hears, Mary retains them and reflects on them in a way that leads her to deeper understanding. By meditating on these mysteries, Mary is able to perceive their deeper meanings and their implications for her life.

Because Mary is the only adult in the infancy narrative to play a role in the later Gospel, she forms a bridge between the infancy narrative and the ministry of Jesus. She will continue to ponder the words and events of her life throughout the ministry of Jesus and she will continue to interpret them with the community of disciples after the resurrection. As the model disciple she is one of those who "hear the word of God and observe it" (11:28).

Luke 2:21 The Circumcision and Naming of Jesus

21When eight days were completed for his circumcision, he was named Jesus, the name given him by the angel before he was conceived in the womb.

The birth, the circumcision and naming, and the manifestation of Jesus are all closely related and parallel the same events in the account of John the Baptist. The narrative is deeply rooted in the ancient traditions of the Torah.

59

Circumcised on the eighth day, Jesus is marked with the sign of the covenant (Gen 17:11) and is incorporated into the people of Israel. The text, however, stresses the significance of the naming of Jesus. Luke does not explain the meaning of the name of Jesus as does Matthew 1:21, though clearly Luke understands that salvation is expressed in the name. Luke, rather, emphasizes that the naming fulfills God's will as expressed through the command of Gabriel at the Annunciation (1:31).

Luke 2:22-38 The Presentation in the Temple

[22]When the days were completed for their purification according to the law of Moses, they took him up to Jerusalem to present him to the Lord, [23]just as it is written in the law of the Lord, "Every male that opens the womb shall be consecrated to the Lord," [24]and to offer the sacrifice of "a pair of turtledoves or two young pigeons," in accordance with the dictate in the law of the Lord.

[25]Now there was a man in Jerusalem whose name was Simeon. This man was righteous and devout, awaiting the consolation of Israel, and the holy Spirit was upon him. [26]It had been revealed to him by the holy Spirit that he should not see death before he had seen the Messiah of the Lord. [27]He came in the Spirit into the temple; and when the parents brought in the child Jesus to perform the custom of the law in regard to him, [28]he took him into his arms and blessed God, saying:

[29]"Now, Master, you may let your servant go in peace, according to your word,
[30]for my eyes have seen your salvation,
[31] which you prepared in sight of all the peoples,
[32]a light for revelation to the Gentiles,
  and glory for your people Israel."

[33]The child's father and mother were amazed at what was said about him; [34]and Simeon blessed them and said to Mary his mother, "Behold, this child is destined for the fall and rise of many in Israel, and to be a sign that will be contradicted [35](and you yourself a sword will pierce) so that the thoughts of many hearts may be revealed." [36]There was also a prophetess, Anna, the daughter of Phanuel, of the tribe of Asher. She was advanced in years, having lived seven years with her husband after her marriage, [37]and then as a widow until she was eighty-four. She never left the temple, but worshiped night and day

with fasting and prayer. [38]And coming forward at that very time, she gave thanks to God and spoke about the child to all who were awaiting the redemption of Jerusalem.

The journey "up to Jerusalem" was traveled often by faithful Israelites. Entry into the courts of the Temple, the focal point of Israel's memories and hopes, was the climax of this religious pilgrimage. The journey shows that the beginning of Jesus' life was set completely within Judaism, and it anticipates the final journey of Jesus in the Gospel toward his destiny in Jerusalem, the city of salvation.

The family of Jesus faithfully observed the Law of Moses. Five times in this narrative Luke observes that they did everything required by the Law (2:22, 23, 24, 27, 39). This observance included the law regarding circumcision, purification of the mother, and presentation of the firstborn. The Law, the Temple, and the spirit of prophecy, all ancient expressions of the covenant, come together to form the context of God's new revelation.

Luke sketchily refers in verses 22-24 to two separate regulations: the purification of the mother after the birth of a child (Lev 12:1-8) and the dedication of the firstborn son to God (Exod 13:2, 12-16). The purification of the woman was to be completed forty days after the birth of a male child. Only then could she reenter the court of women on the Temple mount. She was to bring an offering of a lamb as well as a pigeon or turtledove to be offered by the Temple priest so that she would be "clean again after her flow of blood" (Lev 12:7). If she could not afford a lamb, however, she could bring two pigeons or turtledoves. This offering of the poor expressed Mary's obedience to the Law.

The Law stated that every firstborn male, whether human or animal, belonged to God who saved Israel's firstborn when the firstborn of Egypt died. The firstborn son was to be dedicated to the service of God. Yet, the parents could release the child from this demand of the Law by a symbolic act of redemption. This ransom or buying back was made by paying five silver shekels (Num 18:15-16). The narrative does not indicate, however, that Jesus was redeemed, hinting at his lifelong consecration to God's service.

The account of the presentation of Jesus imitates the account of Samuel's dedication to God at the Temple in Shiloh (1 Sam 1:24-28). Samuel's parents, Hannah and Elkanah, took their child up to the Temple to offer him to God's service. The encounter of Mary and

Joseph with the elderly Simeon continues to echo the Samuel story. At the Temple the parents of Samuel encountered the elderly priest, Eli. They presented him with the offerings for sacrifice and he blessed them, just as Simeon blesses Joseph and Mary (2:34).

Simeon personifies ancient Israel, filled with expectant hope. In this old man Israel acknowledges the end of a long wait and the beginning of a new age of God's salvation. The old Israel could now rest in peace as the new, messianic age of Israel arose. The description of Simeon, "awaiting the consolation of Israel," echoes the language of the second part of the Book of Isaiah (40–66), often called the Book of Consolation. The work begins with God's words of consolation: "Comfort, give comfort to my people." God proclaims to Jerusalem that she is forgiven of her sins and her time of service is at an end (Isa 40:1-2). The work concludes with a final declaration of God's consolation for Jerusalem as she gives birth to God's renewed people: "As a mother comforts her son, so will I comfort you; in Jerusalem you shall find your comfort" (Isa 66:13).

Three times the text indicates that the Holy Spirit was upon Simeon (2:25, 26, 27). The Holy Spirit had revealed to him that he would not die until he had seen God's Messiah. He was moved by the Spirit to go to the Temple at the hour Jesus was being presented, and in the Spirit he knew that the child was the consolation and salvation of Israel.

This devout old man, ready to die, holds the six-week-old infant in his arms as he praises God for keeping his Word. The Canticle of Simeon announces that the moment which explains his whole life has now come. Like a loyal sentinel, he had kept watch all his life in expectation of the Lord's coming. Now at this turning point of history, he could be dismissed as he welcomes the salvation of all peoples.

As Israel was ready to die after he had looked upon the face of his lost son Joseph (Gen 46:30), so also Simeon is prepared to die now that he has seen the fulfillment of God's promise in Jesus. As the eyes of Simeon look upon the world's salvation (2:30), the scene anticipates the fulfillment of Isaiah's prophecy proclaiming that all people will see the salvation of God (Isa 40:5; 52:10). This sense of fulfillment is expressed in the words of Jesus during his journey to Jerusalem: "Blessed are the eyes that see what you see . . . Many prophets and kings desired to see what you see" (10:23-24).

The canticle proclaims salvation for all the people of the earth, the Gentiles as well as the people of Israel (2:32). This universality of

God's saving will had already been expressed in the Old Testament. God had promised to Abraham that all the nations of the earth would find blessing (Gen 22:18); in the Isaian writings God announced "a light for the nations" and that "salvation may reach to the ends of the earth" (Isa 42:6; 49:6).

This proclamation of the universal significance of Jesus, which brought amazement to Mary and Joseph, anticipates the intention of the entire Gospel and Acts. The ministry of Jesus and the early Church will make clear that Jews and Gentiles together make up God's people. Simeon expresses the understanding that will be later proclaimed by the principal heroes of the early Church. Peter proclaimed in the climactic scene of Acts that the Gentiles have heard the Gospel and believed (Acts 15:7, 14); Paul proclaimed at the end of Acts, "Let it be known to you that this salvation of God has been sent to the Gentiles" (Acts 28:28). The advent of universal salvation is announced from the beginning to the end of the writings of Luke.

After the canticle Simeon speaks directly to Mary in the form of a prophetic oracle (2:34-35). In the midst of this narrative filled with light, joy, and hope, a dark shadow is cast. Simeon specifies that the consolation of Israel and the salvation of the Gentiles will not occur without great cost. Like a true prophet he sees the actions of God as well as the tragedy of human choices.

Simeon prophesied that Jesus is "destined for the fall and rise of many in Israel." The truth of Jesus is destined to create a crisis of decision within people. Falling and rising express the centrally important movement of a person's life, either away from or toward God's offer of salvation. The division between those who fall and those who rise is announced in the later preaching of Jesus: "Do you think I have come to establish peace on the earth? No, I tell you, but rather division . . . ." (12:51).

Simeon also prophesied that Jesus is destined to be "a sign that will be contradicted." The "sign" of the nativity, the infant wrapped in cloths and lying in a manger, will lead to the sign of Jesus crucified and buried. He will be a sign that will evoke a divided response; he will be spurned and rejected as well as received and accepted. "The thoughts of many hearts will be revealed" because the people's response to God's Word, either opposition or acceptance, will be made clear in salvation's light.

Simeon's aside to Mary, "and you yourself a sword will pierce," expresses the price she will pay for her intimate association with her

63

son. She too will experience heart-rending pain as she shares in the rejection and suffering of Jesus, both as his mother and as his disciple. She, who was the first to hear and receive the good news about Jesus, must also encounter within her own soul the tragedy of the rejection of that saving news by many.

Through Simeon's prophetic oracle, Luke has introduced the scandal of the cross into the infancy account, as Matthew introduced it with the account of Herod and his slaughter of the children. The shadow of the cross falls upon Luke's whole account, from the infancy narrative through the trials and persecution of the early Church.

Anna is a faithful woman of Israel who, like Simeon, has lived many years. She is the only woman in the New Testament called a prophet, though there are other references to women prophesying (Acts 2:17; 21:9). She takes her place in the Scriptures alongside the other women of Israel who are described as prophets: Miriam (Exod 15:20), Deborah (Judg 4:4), Huldah (2 Kgs 22:14), and Isaiah's wife (Isa 8:3).

She is a woman closely associated with the Temple, the symbol of Israel's hope. She too comes when Jesus is being presented and recognizes that the "redemption of Jerusalem" is at hand. She gives thanks to God and begins to speak about the child to all God's waiting people. She is the final witness in the infancy narrative to speak about the saving significance of Jesus.

Simeon and Anna represent Israel at its best—devout and righteous, moved by God's Spirit, at home in the Temple, longing for the fulfillment of God's promises, waiting for the advent of God's salvation. God's new work is the fulfillment of an old promise; hope is always built on memory.

Luke's description of Jesus' infancy began with an elderly, obedient man and woman, Zechariah and Elizabeth, and it ends with an elderly, obedient man and woman, Simeon and Anna. Both Zechariah and Simeon are filled with the Holy Spirit and chant their canticles in praise of God; both Elizabeth and Anna express joyful thanks to God at the good news that God's salvation has come.

Luke 2:39-40 The Return to Nazareth

39When they had fulfilled all the prescriptions of the law of the Lord, they returned to Galilee, to their own town of Nazareth. 40The child grew and became strong, filled with wisdom; and the favor of God was upon him.

The concluding note of the narrative of Jesus' infancy forms a transition to the years of his childhood and to his adult ministry. Nazareth of Galilee is the town where Jesus will be raised and in which his public life will begin. It is built on the side of a hill which commands a view of the entire Valley of Jezreel, dividing Galilee from Samaria. Mount Tabor and Mount Carmel can also be seen from Nazareth. Jesus grew up with a panorama of reminders of the ancient history of his people.

Luke notes that Jesus grew; he became strong; he was filled with wisdom; and the favor of God was upon him. Like other children of God's promise, Isaac (Gen 21:8), Samuel (1 Sam 2:21, 26), and John (1:80), Jesus grew up in stature and in God's favor. The spirit of wisdom is an attribute of God which was expected to rest upon the Messiah (Isa 11:2). The wisdom of Jesus will be displayed in the next episode as he sits among the teachers in the Temple. Toward the end of his life, Jesus promises to share wisdom with his disciples during the coming persecutions (21:15). The "favor" or "grace" of God which was claimed of Mary (1:30) and of Jesus in the infancy account will become for the Church the favor/grace of the Lord Jesus (Acts 15:11).

Luke 2:41-52 The Boy Jesus in the Temple

[41]Each year his parents went to Jerusalem for the feast of Passover, [42]and when he was twelve years old, they went up according to festival custom. [43]After they had completed its days, as they were returning, the boy Jesus remained behind in Jerusalem, but his parents did not know it. [44]Thinking that he was in the caravan, they journeyed for a day and looked for him among their relatives and acquaintances, [45]but not finding him, they returned to Jerusalem to look for him. [46]After three days they found him in the temple, sitting in the midst of the teachers, listening to them and asking them questions, [47]and all who heard him were astounded at his understanding and his answers. [48]When his parents saw him, they were astonished, and his mother said to him, "Son, why have you done this to us? Your father and I have been looking for you with great anxiety." [49]And he said to them, "Why were you looking for me? Did you not know that I must be in my Father's house?" [50]But they did not understand what he said to them. [51]He went down with them and came to Nazareth, and was obedient to them;

and his mother kept all these things in her heart. [52]And Jesus advanced [in] wisdom and age and favor before God and man.

This narrative is the only account of Jesus' adolescence in the four Gospels. In other Greek biographies of this period, such stories of a hero's youth, giving glimpses of his future significance, appear frequently. Likewise, the Jewish literature of the New Testament period emphasizes the boyhood of biblical characters such as Moses and Samuel, and attributes to them extraordinary knowledge and understanding at an early age. Boyhood accounts of Jesus also increased later and were commonly expressed in the apocryphal gospels.

For Luke, this account is transitional; it creates a less abrupt movement from infancy to adulthood as here Jesus speaks for the first time about himself. The account stands between the revelation about Jesus by others during the conception and birth accounts and the revelation that Jesus himself will proclaim throughout his public ministry.

This final episode of Luke's overture is rightly considered part of the infancy account since, like the conception and birth narratives, it is essentially a revelation of the identity of Jesus. Also, like the other accounts of the infancy, it looks backward to the traditions of Israel and foreshadows essential elements of the public, adult ministry of Jesus.

Throughout the infancy account Jesus has been shown to embody the tradition of Israel. He was brought up in the ritual and moral life of Judaism, and every aspect of his life was in continuity with the best in Judaism. He was circumcised on the eighth day and was presented and dedicated to God in the Temple in his infancy. He was raised within a Jewish home, prayed in the synagogue, and followed the traditions associated with the Temple. Now Jesus, at the age of twelve, was considered by Jewish custom as ready to accept responsibility for the Torah and its moral and ritual commands.

The annual pilgrimage up to Jerusalem for the feast of Passover was the most important of the religious journeys prescribed in the Torah. Joseph and Mary traveled for the feast each year, and Jesus, in obedience to them and in obedience to God's Law, went also. For all faithful Jews the Temple was the center of God's presence and the focus of their worship. Jesus' visit to the Temple expresses his conscious and growing dedication to the will of God.

Pilgrims usually traveled together for company and for safety. Joseph, Mary, and Jesus traveled in a caravan along with their relatives and neighbors from the village of Nazareth. In such a large traveling group, it is not surprising that an adolescent, expected to be traveling with the extended family, would be missing for a day. The frantic search that followed and the reprimand of Jesus by his mother are also expected responses to the loss of a child in a large city.

Luke's model for this account is the Old Testament account of Samuel. The parents of Samuel used to go up once a year to worship God at the Temple in Shiloh. Samuel had been dedicated to God by his mother Hannah from his birth, and as a young boy he was taken by his parents to live permanently at God's Temple in Shiloh. As a youth Samuel received his call from God and came to understand his special mission (1 Sam 3). Josephus, a Jewish historian who lived in the first century, dates the call of Samuel in the Temple to his twelfth year. Jesus, too, since he was dedicated to God's service, belonged to God and would be expected to discern God's call in the Temple.

Like the other accounts within the infancy narrative, this brief account of Jesus' youth contains many elements which anticipate the rest of the Gospel of Luke, especially the passion, death, resurrection, and ascension. This journey of Jesus from Galilee to Jerusalem for the Passover prepares for the journey of his entire life. The major journey of the Gospel begins when Jesus "resolutely determined to journey to Jerusalem" (9:51), and it concludes as Jesus enters the city of his destiny and celebrates the Passover, which will also be the passover of his death and resurrection.

The journey of Jesus to Jerusalem, both in his youth and in the heart of his adult life, culminates in the Temple. This is the place where Jesus first revealed his divine sonship (2:49), and it is the place where Jesus will complete his teaching ministry (20–21). In the Temple at twelve years of age, Jesus seems to be both a learner and a teacher: "All who heard him were astounded at his understanding and his answers" (2:47). His insight and wise discernment anticipates the amazement at his teaching that will mark his entire public life, especially his final teaching in the Temple before his passion.

The loss of the child Jesus and his finding after three days (2:46) anticipates the accomplishment of Jesus' saving deeds in his death and resurrection. Throughout his Gospel Luke associates being lost with death and being found with coming back to life. This is especially clear at the conclusion of Jesus' parable of the lost son. In speaking about what has happened to his son, the father says that he "was dead and has come back to life again; he was lost and has been found" (15:32).

The interval between Jesus' being lost and being found is "three days." This period suggests the interval between his death and burial and his resurrection to life. The loss of Jesus in Jerusalem created confusion and anxiety, just as his death and the report of his resurrection aroused a similar response among his disciples at the end of the Gospel. Yet, the child Jesus explained that his absence from his family and his presence in the Temple was a matter of divine necessity (2:49). This sense of divine destiny is expressed by Jesus throughout the Gospel, especially in reference to the necessity of his death and resurrection (9:22; 24:7, 26). It is based in the saving will of God which Jesus wisely understands through interpreting the Scriptures and which he obediently follows.

All who read the Gospel must come to realize that they too are lost, that they are dead and in need of salvation. The mission of Jesus is to search for those who are lost and dead in sin and to bring them to salvation and life: "The Son of Man has come to seek and to save what was lost" (19:10). With Jesus as the model for all disciples, God's saving will gives direction and a goal for all who follow in his way.

The response of Jesus is the center of this boyhood narrative: "Did you not know that I must be in my Father's house?" (2:49). The meaning is ambiguous in the Greek text; in fact, the word "house" is not found there. Other possible translations include "involved in my Father's affairs/business" and "about my Father's work." However the phrase is translated, the response of Jesus declares that the purpose and goal of his life is in relationship to his Father and in obedience to his will.

Because Luke understands that the ultimate destiny of Jesus requires his being with the Father, these words of Jesus also prepare for the end of the Gospel when Jesus ascends to heaven. The whole life of Jesus is a passage to the Father. The ultimate meaning of his life transcends this world and human history. Even as Jesus is found in the Temple, he has already begun the process of withdrawing from his earthly origins so that he could fulfill his destiny. Likewise, when Jesus withdraws from his disciples and ascends into heaven, his transcendent presence among them becomes even more powerful and effective.

For the first time in the Gospel, Jesus calls God "my Father." Previously his unique relationship with God had been expressed by others: Gabriel, Elizabeth, Mary, Zechariah, Simeon. Jesus expresses in his own words his identity proclaimed by God's messenger at the annunciation: He will be called "the Son of God" (1:35), and the identity to be announced by the heavenly voice at his baptism: "You are my beloved Son" (3:22). Luke continues to affirm the divine nature of Jesus from the beginnings of his earthly life. The Church's proclamation of Jesus as Messiah, Savior, Lord, and Son of God, which was fully understood after the resurrection, is expressed by Luke in the period of his conception, birth, and childhood. Luke shows the essential continuity from the infant Jesus, to the boy Jesus, to the adult ministering Jesus, to the risen Jesus.

As the infancy account concludes, Jesus is shown undoubtedly as the Son of God and Son of Mary. In the advent of the Savior, earth and heaven meet. Jesus went back to Nazareth with Mary and Joseph and was obedient to them (2:51), yet he was also the obedient Son of his heavenly Father. Observance of the Torah, growing in the understanding of Israel's wisdom, faithfulness to the feasts and worship of his people—these form the context for his whole life. Through them Jesus came to fully understand and embrace the purpose and goal of his life as Savior, yet he would save his people in a way that fulfilled and transcended the Temple and institutions of Israel.

Mary, Luke's model of Christian discipleship, did not understand what Jesus said about directing his life to the Father (2:50), yet she "kept all these things in her heart" (2:51). Though she was unable to fully understand the implications of Jesus' identity, she accepted the mystery of his words and his life in the same way that she accepted the mystery of his birth—"Mary kept all of these things, reflecting on them in her heart" (2:19).

Luke encourages all his readers to imitate Mary in the way of discipleship. Those who follow Jesus Christ will not be able to understand all the words he speaks, yet retaining them and reflecting on them will allow the disciple to perceive deeper meanings and the implications for their lives. True disciples are like those in the parable of the sower whose seed falls on rich soil: "They are the ones who, when they have heard the word, embrace it with a generous and good heart, and bear fruit through perseverance" (8:15).